A MATHEMATICAL FRAMEWORK FOR MODELING LEGAL REASONING THROUGH CONDITIONAL LOGIC

A MATHEMATICAL FRAMEWORK FOR
MODELING LEGAL REASONING THROUGH CONDITIONAL LOGIC
Second Edition

Samuel M. Brasil Jr.
Associate Justice,
Espirito Santo State Supreme Court

A FHE PRESS PUBLICATION

Published by FHE Press, Miami, Florida.
Published simultaneously in United States, United Kingdom, Germany, France, Spain, Italy, Japan.

FHE Press also publishes its books in a variety of electronic formats. Some content that appears in print,
however, may not be available in electronic format.

Library of Congress Cataloging-in-Publication Data:

A Mathematical Framework for Modeling Legal Reasoning through Conditional Logic / Samuel M. Brasil Jr.
     p. cm.—(FHE Press series in Artificial Intelligence)
  "FHE Press."
  Includes bibliographical references and index.
  ISBN 978-1-7339642-2-7 (pbk.)
  1. Legal—Reasoning. 2. Artificial—Intelligence.
  —Mathematics. I. Brasil Jr, Samuel M. II. Series.

Printed in the United States of America.

10 9 8 7 6 5 4 3 2 1

To Anna Lara,
Arthur and Henrique

CONTENTS IN BRIEF

1 Foundations of Legal Reasoning   1

2 Nonmonotonic Reasoning   33

3 Conditional Logics and Legal Reasoning   59

4 A Mathematical Environment   89

5 Conclusion   103

CONTENTS

List of Figures   xi

Acknowledgments   xiii

Introduction   xv

1   Foundations of Legal Reasoning   **1**

    1.1   Logics and Legal Reasoning   1

         1.1.1   An Overview on Logic   2

    1.2   Legal Theory and Legal Reasoning   7

         1.2.1   Statutory and Jurisprudential Law   7

         1.2.2   The Concept and Validity of Law   10

         1.2.3   Including Arguments in a Legal System   19

    1.3   Uncertainty in Law   20

         1.3.1   Prima-Facie and All-Things-Considered Obligations   21

         1.3.2   The Theory of Transformation in Law   22

         1.3.3   The Concept of Coherence   25

    1.4   Priority between Normative Propositions   27

         1.4.1   Meta-rules for the Conflict between Norms   27

| | 1.4.2 | Weighing and Balancing | 29 |

2 Nonmonotonic Reasoning — **33**

2.1	A Conceptual Sketch on Nonmonotonic Reasoning	33
	2.1.1	On Certainty and Belief	35
	2.1.2	Nonmonotonic Systems	38
	2.1.3	Non-monotonic Logics	43
	2.1.4	Semantics: fixed-point or model-theoretic?	50
2.2	Model-theoretic semantics and Conditional Logics	51
	2.2.1	Metatheoretic properties	51
	2.2.2	Ranking Functions and Kappa Calculus	53
	2.2.3	Some model-preference systems	54

3 Conditional Logics and Legal Reasoning — **59**

3.1	Semantics for Legal Reasoning	59
	3.1.1	Language and Notation	59
	3.1.2	System Z	60
	3.1.3	Lexicographic Closure	63
3.2	Extending the Semantics	65
	3.2.1	Variable Strength Conditionals	67
	3.2.2	System Z^+ and ε-consistent Knowledge Bases	67
	3.2.3	A New Semantics: System Lex^+	70
3.3	Modeling Legal Reasoning with Conditional Logics	72
	3.3.1	Basic Framework	72
	3.3.2	Modeling Collision Meta-rules	74
	3.3.3	Weighing and Balancing	78
	3.3.4	Alexy's Weight Formula	82
	3.3.5	Legal, Social and Ethical Validity through Lex^+ Semantics	84

4 A Mathematical Environment — **89**

4.1	Introduction	89
4.2	The Maximum Satisfiability Problem	90
4.3	A Mathematical Framework for Lex^+ Semantics	92
4.4	Tractability of Conditional Logics	100

5 Conclusion — **103**

LIST OF FIGURES

1.1   Kelsen's Hierarchical Structure of the Legal System (Stufenbau)   14

1.2   Frame generated by a higher norm   28

2.1   Example of Inheritance Network   40

2.2   Ranking Function   54

3.1   The Ranking $k^z(w_i)$ for the trespass example.   62

3.2   The *Lex*-tuples for the trespass example.   65

3.3   The Ranking $k^+(w_i)$ for the trespass example.   69

3.4   The Lex^+-tuples for the trespass example.   72

ACKNOWLEDGMENTS

- A special word of thanks goes to Prof. Dr. Berilhes Borges Garcia[1], my Advisor at the Master's Program in Computer Science. Without his guidance, this work would not be possible.

- I would also like to thank Prof. Dr. Raul Henrique Cardoso Lopes[2] and Prof. Dr. Flavio Miguel Varejao[3] for their priceless discussion and contribution to my work.

- I'm also deeply indebted my family, parents, colleagues and friends for their support and encouragement.

Samuel M. Brasil Jr

---

[1] https://inf.ufes.br/ berilhes/
[2] https://inf.ufes.br/ raulh/
[3] https://inf.ufes.br/ fvarejao/

INTRODUCTION

This book is an interdisciplinary study in Civil Procedural Law (Judicial Decision-making) and Artificial Intelligence. It is the result of my research at the Federal University of Espirito Santo when I was pursuing my Master's degree in Computer Science. It is actually a revised version of my original thesis defended as capstone unity of the Master's program. My thesis was written in 2002/2003, and first published in 2004. Papers with parts of this work were published both in 2002 and 2003 (Garcia and Brasil [2002a], Brasil and Garcia [2003]). I did not make any modifications to the current version of the thesis to preserve its original content. The only changes I have made were to correct the grammar and some typos.

On Legal Reasoning

It should be noted that Legal Reasoning has challenged logicians and philosophers from the very beginning, over the task of representing legal knowledge and modeling its reasoning procedure. In the early 1800s, the major approach to legal systems was based on the deductive aspect of classical logic, in a movement known in German as *begriffsjurisprudenz* (jurisprudence of concepts). However, this formal way of thinking in respect to legal reasoning was not unanimous in the literature. Some authors suggested that different forms of normative theories should be more appropriate. Then, there were *Interessenjurisprudenz, Freie Rechtsfindung, Wienerkreis*, to name but a few trends of normative reasoning. Nevertheless, an adequate method against deductive logic was not introduced at that time and syllogistic reasoning based on general norms and concepts still kept its place, despite its weakness in capturing practical consequences. Around the 1950s, some researchers, like Viehweg [1953], Perelman and Olbrechts-Tyteca [1958], Toulmin [1958], changed the paradigm of the deductive approach claiming that legal reasoning was not logical but rather rhetorical (or argument-based in some sense). Then, topic and argumentation theories were linked again to the reasoning procedure of law. Perelman and Olbrechts-Tyteca [1958] investigated the subject under Frege's formalism and claimed that legal reasoning cannot be captured by a logical model. He claimed that only an argumentation theory could achieve extra-logical values in law, such as social or moral consequences, which is far from the formalism of classical logic. In the core of his theory was the concept of audience, and the arguments have different persuasive strength accordingly to the audience. Toulmin presented an informal model of arguments which has captured the attention of the literature of the past 20 years. Nowadays, we have seen the work of Alexy [1978], McCormick [1978], Peczenik [1989], Aarnio [1987] and others, devoted to expose the argumentative nature of legal reasoning. Actually, deductive approach and formal theories in law, whether or not logic-based, have never had the same performance as argumentation theories, in the task of capturing the behavior of legal reasoning. In recent years, however, we have seen the rising of non-classical logics, such as nonmonotonic reasoning, developed in the Artificial Intelligence field to deal with uncertainty and incomplete information typically found in common sense. These features are also found in legal reasoning and the interrelationship of nonmonotonic logics and law was a natural consequence. It's worth a note that some nonmonotonic formalisms were even inspired by legal reasoning, e.g., Prakken and Sartor [1996], Gordon [1993b], Hage [1997], Verheij [1994], to name but a few. The literature had already introduced some theories translating legal reasoning into a nonmonotonic formalism based on argumentation semantics. With such a translation, an important tool will be available to check out the rationality of legal discourse, and even to enable a framework to compute legal reasoning. Despite the state-of-the-art of these theories, some questions remain claiming further research, such as whether legal reasoning can actually be captured in all its features by a logical formalism that is both complete and sound, and whether legal reasoning is computable. These questions are the main problem of our research. To solve this problem, we aim at presenting a logical translation of legal reasoning based on the nonmonotonic semantics described in the current literature, and also, introducing a mathematical environment to allow for its implementation.

An issue that makes this research worthwhile both to Computer Science and to Legal Theory, lies on the need of formal methods to test correctness. Computer scientists are always concerned not only with complexity, but also with correctness of algorithms. Therefore, formal methods to verify the correctness is not only desired but essential. So, a translation of legal reasoning to a logical framework will be useful for such verification. For Legal Theory, a logical model still keeps its importance, likewise, as long as rationality of legal discourse is desired. Since early Greece, philosophers aimed at finding a correct way of reasoning and in this task, logic has an important role. I should advise that even though I do accept that logic is important to verify the rationality of discourse, I'm not claiming that a legal discourse is 'rational' if and only if it is logically deducible. The assertion for the need of logic for rationality is antisymmetric, and the converse does not hold, since we cannot constraint the concept of rational reasoning by saying that only logical deduction gives rationality. There are other factors such as coherence, reasonability, etc. Anyway, logical deduction is important to the rationality because an argument is only acceptable if it is sound.

As far as I stated that computer scientists are concerned with correctness and also with complexity, a note should be done by the latter. Computational complexity of nonmonotonic logics is increasingly higher compared to monotonic ones. Provable methods of monotonic logics are *local*, i.e., the proof of a theorem will be a part of the knowledge base. When the proof is found, the search can stop. For example, if we are looking for a proof whether τ holds given a fact σ then the proof method can stop as soon as the conditional $\sigma \to \tau$ is found. Nonmonotonic proofs for his turn are *global* and have a completely different behavior, since new evidence can invalidate the proof. Thus, even when the proof method finds the conditional $\sigma \to \tau$ that derives τ, the proof procedure might keep searching. For each conditional added to the inference steps, the entire knowledge base might be inspected since new information can invalidate a nonmonotonic entailment and, therefore, the proof. For this reason, nonmonotonic logic is less tractable than monotonic one. This feature is very important in the argumentation level, and in legal reasoning as well, since we think of argumentation framework as a proof system.

Structure of Book

We start in Chapter I discussing the foundations of Legal Reasoning. So important when modeling legal reasoning is knowing exactly what will be modeled. We do not claim that the legal theory used (and adapted by us) in this work is the only one or the best one. However, it seemed to us to be sufficient to obtain acceptable results. We explain some fundamental concepts in legal reasoning, such as validity, efficacy, and address a fruitful discussion over the clash of norms or arguments.

Chapter II brings a brief review on nonmonotonic logics. Nonmonotonic logics are used as underlying theory e forms the foundation of our approach. The failure of classical first order logic in representing legal reasoning occurs because legal norms are subject to exceptions. In classical logic, the addition of new axioms does not overule a derived theorem. In a word, classical logic is monotonic. Unfortunately, this is not a desired property in Law Theory. Legal reasoning, otherwise, is nonmonotonic since the addition of new information can exclude a consequence of a legal norm.

Thus, a legal rule is only applied in the absence of information showing that the conclusion are found wrong. In this sense, nonmonotonic reasoning seems to be a natural way to formalize legal reasoning. In the first chapter we summarize the language used in this dissertation and the main features of some nonmonotonic logics.

Next, we briefly present three formalisms that are already classical in the field of nonmonotonic research: default logic, circumscription and autoepistemic logic. The remaining sections show the development of two different approaches to nonmonotonic reasoning, that are grouped according to their metatheoretic properties. Logics that keeps metalevel properties such as *cumulativity* and *preferentiality* are based on model-theoretic semantics, while logics formalized without such properties work on fixed-point semantics. We finish the chapter with an overview of computational complexity of nonmonotonic reasoning.

In the next Chapter, we start with a description of legal systems, to situate the reader on the main difference between statutory and jurisprudential law. We are not going in depth with this description, since it is not the scope of this research. The purpose is to allow an insight on the validity of generating legal norms which will be useful through all the theory, on the issue of making default assumptions. Next, a representation of legal reasoning based on deductive logic will be presented. Here, the structure of legal norms will be described, and a formal translation will be introduced. As occurs in current trends of legal logic, we will give an introductory account of modal logic, specially the modal deontic logic, that has the operators "obligated", "forbidden" and "permitted". Although normative reasoning that is based on modal deontic logic may have its proper research field such as modal nonmonotonic logics, a reduction to propositional logic is needed, on an account to maintain the same logical language through all this research. Such a conversion will then be introduced. Forwarding, the problem of natural interpretation of legal norms will be analyzed, and the syntactical, semantical and pragmatical consequences of legal interpretation will be pointed out. A model of interpretation based on set theory and higher order logic will be suggested, to enable a formal interpretation based on models. Then, we will introduce a logical translation of legal reasoning using a model-theoretic semantics. A conditional logic is used so that the theory can entail legal sentences that are *sound*.

Since we also investigated logics that are noncumulative, a fixed-point semantics to legal reasoning will be presented in Chapter III. This approach is related to argumentation systems. We start by presenting a discussion over justification-based approach of legal reasoning, which differs in the matter from conditional logics. Justification-based reasoning uses argumentation systems as inference procedure to derive sentences that are entailed. If an inference procedure finds a proof of entailed sentences, specifying the reasoning steps that are sound, then it is *complete*. So, the completeness of the theory will be reached by an argumentation proof method. In Law, justification of legal sentences is essential so that one can verify whether the decision is sound. The main non-formal theories on legal argumentation will be discussed, so also will be the formal ones, that were developed especially for legal reasoning. A relevant issue in legal argumentation theory is the strength of arguments. At this point we need to provide a warning. In this Chapter we will also examine the logical structure of some legal arguments to elucidate their *persuasive* strength. Although the efforts over the subject we will neither present a criterion of strength of the specific legal arguments described here, nor an ordering among them. The scope of the section remains only to point out the behavior of legal arguments in an argumentation procedure. We finish the chapter with a logical translation of legal reasoning using a fixed-point semantics, that are based on argumentation theories.

Using model-theoretic semantics of conditional logic and also fixed-point semantics of defeasible argumentation to set out the legal reasoning framework, we shall introduce complete and sound legal reasoning.

As soon as a formalism to legal reasoning is satisfactorily introduced, a still more difficult question arises. Implementing inference procedures in classical logic is a hard task, and implementing a logical formalism that deals with non-classical features, such as nonmonotonic reasoning and legal reasoning, will substantially increase the problem. The core of this problem rests on the complexity to deal with nonmonotonic logics and, therefore, with legal reasoning.

So, as important as finding a logical model for legal reasoning is finding a framework to implement it. Chapter IV is devoted to introducing such framework, in a mathematical environment. We start with a brief discussion over satisfiability in mathematical programming and, next, we introduce a translation of the model-theoretic semantics to a mathematical programming environment. Finally, we review the complexity problem of nonmonotonic reasoning.

The conclusion cites practical results of this experiment. We have used LINDO to process the algorithms.

CHAPTER 1

FOUNDATIONS OF LEGAL REASONING

"Δικαια μεν... λεγοντες πολλοι αδικα ποιουισι."
(Saying righteous things, many do unrighteous things).

—Xenofonte, *Memorabilia* (4, 4, 10)

1.1 Logics and Legal Reasoning

Logic is no more an exclusive matter of philosophers and mathematicians. Rather, logic is ubiquitous and the logical inference procedures play an important role in applied sciences, including Computer Science and Law.

Reasoning is an act of thinking where inferences are made or where conclusions are derived from a given set of premisses[1]. As pointed out by Copi [1961], not all thought can be considered as a reasoning, but all reasoning is a kind of thought. For instance, we can think in a number among 1 and 10 without reasoning about it.

---

[1]Following C. S. Peirce and others, I shall adopt the spelling *premiss* and its plural *premisses* for the logical term to distinguish it from *premise* in other senses, in particular to distinguish it from the legal term *premises*.

However, to derive a number from a sum or from a multiplication we need to reason about it. To summarize, we can say that reasoning is the ability to draw conclusions from a set of premises. In logic, such derivability involves adopting a particular formal language. Logic is usually concerned with the analysis of sentences and their proof, paying attention to the *form* instead of to the *substance*. But this does not mean ignoring the semantics of a logical system. Actually, one should recognize the necessity of sound inference procedures. Let us take two examples to illustrate it:

■ EXAMPLE 1.1   Church [1956]

> I have seen a portrait of John Wilkes Booth; John Wilkes Booth assassinated Abraham Lincoln; therefore, I have seen a portrait of the assassin of Abraham Lincoln.

■ EXAMPLE 1.2   Church [1956]

> I have seen a portrait of somebody; somebody invented the wheeled vehicle; therefore, I have seen a portrait of an inventor of the wheeled vehicle.

The reasoning steps expressed on both arguments are the same. However, the argument 1.1 is intuitively valid, while the argument 1.2 is rather invalid. This occurs because the word *somebody* is too vague and ambiguous to be related to the same object in the world[2]. Hence, logical analysis should also be concerned to the soundness of sentences, that is, the corresponding representation of the world.

Thus, what characterizes reasoning is the ability to derive sentences from a knowledge base, keeping the completeness and the soundness of the reasoning procedure.

1.1.1   An Overview on Logic

In ancient Greece, many philosophers emphasized the importance of correct reasoning, requiring an axiomatic method to validate theorems by deduction from axioms. The remarkable work of Aristotle (384-322 b.C.), compiled in the so-called *Organon* and formed by the books *Categoriae, De Interpretatione, Analytica Priora, Analytica Posteriora, Topica* and *De Sophistics Elenchis*, is an example of a step toward a calculus of reasoning that had prestige over the literature for centuries, though it is now outdated by modern mathematical logic. Aristotle was the first to introduce a Predicate Calculi, with the quantifiers "all" and "some", translated in modern terminology to "for all" and "there exists". He was also the first to introduce modal logics, based on the operators *it is possible that p* and *it is necessary that p*. And his syllogism was used for a long time in the curriculum of several colleges, with the purpose of eliminating incorrect reasoning.

It is not the scope of this dissertation to provide a detailed analysis of the work of Aristotle (for a different view of what Aristotle did, see Lukasiewicz [1957]),

---

[2]A syntactical solution is given by assigning to the term in both premises different symbols.

but only to point out the importance of a method to ensure the correctness of exact reasoning. And undoubtedly logic is such a method.

Leibniz (1666), for instance, was convinced that a calculus of reasoning could be developed, in what he called "lingua characteristica" (universal language) and the "calculus ratiocinator" (calculus of reasoning). He claimed that *"humanity would have a new kind of an instrument increasing powers of reason far more than any optical instrument has ever aided the power of vision"* (apud Gödel [1944]). However, as a tool to correct reasoning in lieu of Leibniz's Dream or not, logics is very suitable to provide a method to formal verification of correctness of reasoning.

Logical methods had a significant development in the nineteenth century and forward, on account of the efforts to establish the foundations of mathematical logic, under De Morgan (1847, 1864), Boole (1847, 1854), Peirce (1867, 1880), Schröder (1877, 1890-1905), Frege (1893, 1903), Peano (1894-1908), Whitehead and Russell (1910-1913) and several others. Logics as we know today are not the same as developed by Aristotle. Nevertheless, its importance as a method of correct reasoning was always acknowledged since early Greece.

1.1.1.1 *Knowledge Representation and Logic*

Knowledge can be expressed in a formal language. Such a formal language should also carry on the reasoning procedure, to determine what follows from the knowledge base by means of an inference mechanism.

Statements of facts, properties, relations, and thus state-of-affairs can be represented by means of a logical language, if it is expressive enough. There are several ways of representing them logically, according to the logical systems described in the literature. It may be interesting to give a rough classification of the logics that use classical paradigm, even though the number of non-classical logics increases ceaseless.

Classical propositional logic is a logic of compound sentences formed with connectives such as $\wedge$, $\vee$, $\rightarrow$, and $\neg$, standing for *and, or, if-then* and *not*, respectively. This system is neither concerned with the properties of the sentences nor the quantifiers. Usually, propositions have been burdened with multiple roles, as truth bearers, as sentence meanings, as objects of propositional attitudes. One must be aware, according to Spohn [1994], that no entity can actually play all these roles, though it is unclear how to characterize the appropriate entities for each one.

When one uses the notion of a property or a relation between objects in the representation, one has First Order Predicate Logic. Thus, First Order Predicate Logic allows to quantify over objects, that is, the first-order entities that exist in the world. In FOPL, one uses the quantifiers $\forall$ and $\exists$, standing for *for all* and *there exists*. Notice that what characterizes a property or a relation is the arity of the predicate. A binary predicate expresses a relation, e.g., for a proposition ϕ meaning *marriage*, $\phi(x, y)$ denotes "x is married with y". A unary predicate expresses a property, e.g., one may use $\phi(John, y)$ to denote "John is married with y". A 0-ary predicate expresses a proposition, e.g., $\phi(John, Mary)$ denoting "John is married with Mary". In Predicate Logic, a proposition is a statement of facts that is independent of any variables.

Modal logic extends the vocabulary of classical logic with modal operators such as $\Box$ and $\Diamond$, standing for *it is necessary that* and *it is possible that*, respectively. The semantics of modal logics are built based on Kripke's *many possible worlds* (see Chellas [1980], also with an analysis of deontic logics). There exists a large class of modal logics, depending on the properties assumed by these operators, and the most prominent for legal reasoning is Deontic Logic, which interprets the operators as $\bigcirc$ and P, that is, *it is obligatory that* and *it is permitted that*, respectively. Deontic logic was developed by von Wright [1951], and his works on norms and actions are well known[3].

Higher Order Logic or Type Theory allows not only to quantify over *objects* but over *relations* or *functions* as well. Although higher order logics expressiveness is strictly more powerful than first-order logic, allowing a representation that is not possible in other logical languages, in general case it is undecidable, just like FOPL. There are few logicians with a full understanding on how to reason effectively with sentences in higher-order logic. It deserves to mention the remarkable work of Lopes and Tarver [1997] and Lopes [1999].

One must also be aware of the distinction made by Haack [1996]: some logics can be *extended*, in the sense that they can deal with things that classical logic cannot by extending the basic language of the logic; other logics are *deviant*, in the sense that, although using roughly the same vocabulary as classical logic, they make some of the theorems false where classical logic would have them true. A logic can be both deviant and extended.

Since this work is first concerned with a mathematical model of legal reasoning using conditional logics nonmonotonic systems, the language will be constrained to propositional calculus.

1.1.1.2 *Soundness and Completeness of a Theory*

As we have seen, logic does not operate on the facts themselves but rather on the representation of facts. Logical levels thus are twofold: a syntactical one and its semantical counterpart. The syntactical inference procedure is denoted by $\vdash$, and the semantical inference procedure is denoted by $\vDash$.

A reasoning procedure seeks the construction of new representations of the facts from the old ones, where the formers actually follow from the latter. If the old sentences have true values, the generated new sentences must necessarily have true values. This relation is called *entailment* and is denoted by $\Gamma \vDash \varphi$. On the other hand, an inference procedure can record the steps of entailed sentences. Such procedure is called a *proof* and is denoted by $\Gamma \vdash \varphi$.

So far, an inference procedure not only generates new sentences that are entailed from the old ones, but also report whether or not the new sentences are entailed by the knowledge base, specifying the reasoning steps of the entailed sentences. The

---

[3]Professor von Wright was one of the most important legal philosophers of our time (he died in Helsingfors on June 16), though not a jurist himself. Born in 1916, he studied philosophy under Eino Kaila, the Finnish champion of logical empiricism and member of the Vienna Circle, and later in Cambridge with Broad and Wittgenstein. After Wittgenstein's resignation in 1948 he became his successor in Cambridge, but three years later he returned to Finland to reassume his professorship at the Helsinki University.

former inference procedure is said to be *sound* or *truth-preserving*, while the latter is said to be *complete*. Therefore, a theory is *sound* if and only if every formula provable from the premises is entailed by the premises, or if $\Gamma \vdash \varphi$ then $\Gamma \vDash \varphi$, while it is *complete* if and only if every formula entailed by the premises is provable from the premises, or if $\Gamma \vDash \varphi$ then $\Gamma \vdash \varphi$.

1.1.1.3 *Mathematics, Logics and Legal Reasoning*

Foreseeing a judicial decision was always an old yearning. The mathematician Poisson published in 1837 the *"Recherches sur la probabilité des jugements em matière criminelle et en matière civile"* (Poisson [1837]), introducing a probability calculus to measure the *"espérance mathématique"* of acquitment. In 1875 Condorcet published his *"Essai sur les probabilités en fait de justice"*, also aiming to give a probabilistic measure of judicial decisions. But the aim to foreseen a judicial decision was not restricted to mathematics.

Logics were the main concern of legal philosophers as well and have been investigated from a long time ago. The approach aiming at building a legal concept through logical deduction was investigated by authors of the movement called *begriffjurisprudenz*, as we can see in the work of Puchta [1875]. Other research of significance in legal reasoning are the works of Hohfeld [1923] on legal relations, that was formalized by Lindahl [1977]; the remarkably works of Klug [1966] in the early 50's; the research of Alchourrón and Bulygin [1971] and Alchourrón and Bulygin [1977] on normative systems; Kamlah and Lorenzen [1973] on logical propaedeutic; Tammelo [1978] on proving logical validity and solidity of legal thoughts; Schreiber [1962]; Alchourrón and Makinson [1981]; Åqvist [1977]; Soeteman [1989], McCormick [1978], Peczenik [1989], Atienza [1986] and several others.

Notice that in the beginning, the referred research in the legal logics tried very hard to formalize legal reasoning only in classical logic. There were works proposing the formalization of legal reasoning in propositional calculus, in first order predicate calculus and in modal logic. Almost all of the formalisms also proposed a Deontic extension, since legal reasoning is mainly characterized by the modals *obligatory*, *forbidden* (or *obligatory not*) and *permitted*. To my knowledge, there was no attempt to formalize legal reasoning in higher order logic (type theory). Despite the efforts, there always has been a gap, since the introduced formalisms were not expressive enough to capture legal reasoning patterns.

Nevertheless, in the last 20 years we have seen several works attempting to formalize legal reasoning in extended or in deviant logics, most of them through computer science research in the artificial intelligence field.

1.1.1.4 *Artificial Intelligence and Law*

As early as the appearance of the first computers, legal reasoning has captured the attention of computer scientists and philosophers, settling every one's imagination about the possible use of electronic machines (computers) to obtain a legal consequence or a judicial decision. As events unfold, there were a wide range of researchers who have been working on formalizing legal reasoning in a computer system. The first work on representing law in computer systems that I have information about was from Frank [1949], in what he called '*legal-logic machines*' (see Prakken [1997]). As soon as 1957, Ulrich Klug

(Klug and Fiedler [1964] Klug [1966]) issued a theoretical foundation of such representation, discussing this topic with Norbert Wiener. In that work, Klug had given a sketch of how legal logic can be used in computer systems. So, a fruitful discussion arose in the literature, with important works from Fiedler, that holds PhD both on Law and also on Mathematics (see Fiedler [1962], Fiedler [1964], Fiedler [1966], Fiedler [1968]), and also with the research of Klug and Fiedler [1964] Klug [1966], Bull [1965], Baumgärtel [1972], Steinmüller [1975], among others. In 1963, Viktor Knapp, from University of Plaga, published a paper about cybernetic methods applied to Law (Knapp [1963]). From the late URSS, we find over the subject the work of Andrejew and Kerimow [1960]. However, the paper that is considered by some authors as the first in Artificial Intelligence and Law field was written by Buchanan and Headrick [1970].

In the USA, there were the Journal M.U.L.L. - Modern Uses of Logic in Law (from 1959 to 1966), edited by L.E. Allen, later named 'Jurimetrics Journal', and also 'Law and Computer Technology'. Nowadays, there exists the journal *Artificial Intelligence and Law*, edited by K.D. Ashley, A. Oskamp and G. Sartor, from 1993 on.

The theoretic discussion led toward to the implementation of the projects, and we have seen several works implementing law in computer systems. One of the forerunners systems that aimed to model legal reasoning applying AI techniques was McCarty's TAXMAN project McCarty [1977], implementing statute rules of a subset of American tax law. Several other systems were also developed. Among them: Sergot and Kowalski Sergot [1990], Sergot *et al.* [1986] formalizing law through logic programming techniques; Ashley and Rissland introduced HYPO Ashley and Rissland [1987], which applies legal reasoning using a formalism based on case law decisions; Rissland and Skalak implemented CABARET Rissland and Skalak [1992], which combines HYPO with rule based reasoning; Lodder & Herczog introduced DiaLaw Lodder and Herczog [1995], a dialogical model of legal justification; Gordon's The Pleadings Game Gordon [1993b] and Gordon [1993a], using model-theoretic semantics from Pearl to formalize a legal argumentation system; Gordon and Karacapilidis [1997], on Zeno Argumentation Framework.

Other systems of interest are Prolexs Walker *et al.* [1991], IKBALS Zeleznikov *et al.* [1993], HELIC-II Nitta *et al.* [1995], GREBE (Branting [2000]), which stands for 'Generator of Recursive Exemplar-Based Explanations', a Common Lisp implementation of the framework for integrating legal rules and judicial precedents. Prakken & Sartor developed a remarkable System (informally referred to as PRATOR) Prakken and Sartor [1996], modeling legal reasoning from the language of extended logic programming to that of full first order predicate logic. Jaap Hage introduced RBL (Hage [1997]), which stands for *Reason Based Logic*, a first order predicate logic formalism based on the legal theory of Raz [1975]. Bart Verheij implemented CumulA Verheij [1996], a model of argumentation in stages with application in Law.

Certainly, several systems were omitted, though they are of much significance and interest. Notice that there were also several systems developed not for legal reasoning, but which can be very suitable to such a task, as Pollock's OSCAR or Vreeswijk's Argumentation System Vreeswijk [1993].

In Brazil, there were some works over the subject matter. The first academic research was developed in University of Sao Paulo (USP). In 1973, the Dean of USP, Dr. Miguel Reale, invited Prof. Mario G. Losano from Milan, to make several lectures about computer science and law through all the month of august. The results were presented in a book Garcia [1976]. However, the project was early abandoned. Recently, the University Federal of Santa Catarina (UFSC) has included in the curriculum a course on artificial intelligence and law, under the direction of prof. Aires Jose Rover Rover [2001].

There were also a small research group at FDV Vitoria College of Law in the second semester of 1999, created by the author, to review the existing theories about artificial intelligence and law and the introduced formalisms. In 2000, with the formal admission of the author in the Master's Program in Computer Science at the Federal University of Espirito Santo, there was a research regarding non-monotonic reasoning and Law coordinated by Berilhes Borges Garcia. This research was limited to the Master's program and the results were presented on the Master Thesis delivered on 2002.

The present work is both concerned with the theoretical aspects of legal reasoning and with modeling it in a mathematical environment, which also allows its implementation. We used to refer to the System introduced by this dissertation in our informal talks as CLAIMS, standing for *Converting Legal Arguments Into Max-Sat*.

1.2 Legal Theory and Legal Reasoning

In this Section, I shall briefly discuss about the main properties of the concept and the validity of Law, in the aim at justifying the addition of a legal norm in a legal knowledge base.

1.2.1 Statutory and Jurisprudential Law

The legal systems of western law are mainly divided in two branches. In continental Europe and Countries which follow such legal model (as Brazil does), prevail the *Statute Law*, whilst in Anglo-Saxon cultures, like England and USA, the main system is the *Common Law*[4].

The *Statute Law* is a system where the law is only created by the legislative branch, that is, the law is the result of the volition of the competent organ empowered to prescribe *general* norms, regulating the state of affairs that are considered relevant to the law. Thus, only the statutes enacted by specific empowered organs, i.e., the legislator, can establish the law, that is, settling which behaviors are obligatory, prohibited or permitted. In systems of *Statute Law*, there is no such thing as

---

[4]There exist others legal systems, like the socialist law (extinct Soviet Union), those with strong religious basis (Indian, orient, etc.) and those that are a mixed of *common law* and *statute law*. The reference in this work to only *common law* and *statute law* has not the scope of a critic upon the systems but rather to identify the legitimacy of the organ to create the law.

judicial creation of the law, as it does exist in *Common Law* systems (judge-made law principle). This limitation is due to the Principle of The Separation of Powers. Thus, law is the result of the *enactments of legislature*.

On the other hand, the *Common Law* system is a customary law, i.e., it arises directly from social relations, without any legislative prescription. The law is made by judicial decisions (judges' *summa ratio*). Nowadays, the *Common Law* is understood as a court generated law, since the binding precedent theory obligates the use of the reasons adopted by judges in a previous case in the decision of later cases. The law is thus laid down by the courts, rather than by legislature.

The debate in the literature about which system is better as a legal model, is extensive and passionate. For all, see the work of sir Edward Coke in (Coke [1817]), considered as the *summa* of the Common Law, and the critics from Thomas Hobbes in (Hobbes [1971]). A complete discussion of both systems exceeds the scope of this work. The reference in this work is only necessary to justify the inclusion of certain legal norms as arguments in a legal system Δ.

The distinction between both systems are based on the contrast between the *case relief* and the *statute relief*, where the former is the creation of the law by a judicial decision, while the latter by a *statute*.

The core of Common Law systems is the doctrine of precedents or, in other words, the doctrine of *stare decisis*. The precedents from the superior courts are binding with respect to similar cases, and the inferior courts must apply them. A reported decision in a particular area which has come to be regarded as settling the law of the issue involved is called the *leading case*. Such important cases are used as guidance by lawyers and judges who face similar issues later. For instance, in USA the *leading case* in *tort* cases is Babcock v. Jackson; in the area of abortion, the *leading case* is Roe v. Wade; when is discussed the competence to decree a divorce, the *leading cases* are Williams v. North Carolina (I) and Williams v. North Carolina (II). The *leading case* on judicial control of unconstitutional norms is Marbury v. Madison, which also influenced Brazilian law.

The authority of the *stare decisis*, i.e., the binding force can be either *persuasive*, guiding similar cases without being regarded as settling the law, e.g., the decision of same jurisdiction courts with equal- or lower-level; or *binding authority*, which binds the inferior courts in the case before it. One should distinguish also between *ratio decidendi* (which is called *holding* in USA), and *dictum* (or *obiter dicta*). *Ratio decidendi* is the norm applied in the case (legal principle) that has broader effects, binding the lower courts. The *dictum*, in this turn, are statements merely *persuasive* that are not conclusive to the decision and thus are not binding precedent.

Usually the courts adhere to the precedent, leaving to the appellate court when the case reaches it upon appeal to decide whether the precedent should no longer be followed. However, a court can disregard a binding precedent, thus avoiding its application. In this situation, occurs the *overruling a prior decision*, and the courts may depart from an anachronistic decision expressly. But, the courts usually prefer to honor the doctrine of *stare decisis* preserving the precedent, by careful *distinguishing it away*, rather than overruling a precedent by objectionable decisions. There are not so many cases that are exactly the same as earlier ones, based on the substantive facts.

On the contrary, it is necessary to compare the factual circumstances of prior cases to see whether the issued case is factually comparable. When there exists an exceptional circumstance - which makes the case not factually comparable -, the appellate court (bound to apply a precedent) may distinguish it from those of earlier cases reducing its importance and even making it meaningless, rather than intentionally disregard it. Therefore, the argumentation in court rooms often becomes a comparative factual analysis settling the relevant circumstances.

Notice that, both in USA and in England, the enactments of the legislative branch have priority over the judicial decisions. Thus, although the main features of such legal systems are based on Common Law, a *case law* can be reversed by statute.

The *Common Law* also contrasts with *Equity*. Initially, the equity provided extraordinary remedies (by the court of chancery), providing the appropriate relief when common law remedies were inadequate.

According to Peter Hay (Hay [2002]), the English distinction between proceedings at law and in equity, initially followed by American colonies, was not maintained by all states and, thus, there were not separate courts for equity proceedings. Later on, the two forms of proceedings were merged into a single form of action known as *civil action* (Rule 2 of the Federal Rules of Civil Procedure). However, the distinction between law and equity remains important, and sometimes a right granted by law is not guaranteed for proceedings in equity. So, one should look for the appropriate remedy for the issue. For instance, in the USA, a suit for damages falls under the "law" (7th Amendment), while a claim for specific performance, injunctive relief or a divorce is an equitable remedy.

"Common Law" originally was only referred to the decisional law of the common law courts, but today it is meant to describe "case law", that is, all decisional or judge-made law, encompassing both common law and equity, as opposed to statutory law.

The legal systems of Roman-German roots, which are strongly based on *Statute Law*, are usually designated by *Civil Law*.

The significance of this distinction to the present work comes from the common characteristics of both systems. In *Common Law* systems, the law is authoritatively settled by *Ratio Decidendi* (differing from *Dictum*) of the courts. However, a binding precedent is defeasible, as long as it can be overruled or distinguished due to the substantive facts of the issue. On *Statute Law* the binding force of the law originates from the statute, which can be excluded only by another statute. Usually, in Civil Law systems, a statute cannot be overruled by a judicial decision.

Nevertheless, as far as I see, this feature of statute law is no longer absolute. Even in Civil Law systems a judicial decision can disregard a statute by distinguishing it upon the substantive facts (relevant circumstances) of the case. We can easily find in the jurisprudence a judicial decision yielding an exception clause to the statutes, even though such exception was not foreseen by another statute. For instance, in REsp. 166.363-PE, published in Feb. 14, 2000, the Brazilian Superior Court of Justice recognized an exception to the legal norm DL 911/69. Notice that such exception was not settled by another statute. A different exception (keeping the underpinning reasons) to the same statute can be found in the decision of the same court in

MC 2.779-RJ, published on Dec. 02, 2000. The Federal Supreme Court of Brazil also already established several exceptions to Brazilian statutes, as we can see in the abridgment of law 608, which yields as exception to the Brazilian Penal Code. Moreover, the recent changes on Brazilian law granted binding force to the decisions of the Federal Supreme Court (Stat. 9.868/99 and Federal Constitution) and, in a narrower sense, also to some decisions based on procedural admissibility of lower courts (Federal Rules of Civil Procedure). According to such statutory prescription, a lower court decision can be immediatly reformed by a higher court whenever this decision conflicts with an abridgment of law or a precedent of the same or higher court. This feature detaches the binding nature of judicial decisions of higher courts over inferior courts.

Such duality of creating legal norms by judicial development of the law does not conflict with the legislative competence to enact the law. One can distinguish the norm enacted by the legislator, settling the consequences that should be abstractly applied to all (general norms), and that one created by judges, applying the legal norms already enacted or by selecting the (relevant) factual circumstances that make that case exceptional (individual norms). For a deeper understanding of general and individual norms, see Alexy [1994].

This conclusion leads us to the problem of the validity of the law.

1.2.2   The Concept and Validity of Law

A much debated issue in the literature is the concept "valid law". Without aim at finishing the controversy, I shall discuss the subject matter by distinguishing three different approaches to the validity of law given by the elegant theory of Alexy [1994].

1.2.2.1   The Basic Elements   The concept of law demands at least three elements, related to one another: authoritative *issuance*, social *efficacy* and *correctness* of content Alexy [1994]. Several different systems can be obtained when the concept of law focuses primarily on one of these elements, that is, when one element is emphasized with respect to the others, though not excluding the latter's.

Denying the correctness of content and carrying out mainly the authoritative issuance and the social efficacy, for instance, one will have a positivistic concept of law. Neglecting the issuance and the efficacy and focusing only in the correctness of content, one will reach a purely moral law or the law of reason. Nevertheless, several intermediate concepts of law are possible between these extremes, depending on the acceptance and the strength of each element.

Therefore, in the core of the concept and the validity of law, we have the authoritative issuance, the social efficacy and the correctness of content.

When the concepts of law are mainly oriented toward efficacy, one has sociological and realist legal theories. In sociological theories, the efficacy is an external aspect, while in realist theories it is an internal aspect. According to Alexy [1994], the external aspect focuses on the observable behaviour of the compliance with the norm or the imposition of a sanction in the case of non-compliance. The internal aspect consists in the psychic dispositions (motivation) for compliance with the norm.

Representatives of the former branch are Weber [1978] and Geiger [1947], and of the latter are Bierling [1979] and Luhmann [1972], which proposes a variant of the form of normative expectation of behaviour. Notice that there are combinations of both aspects, as we can see in Ross [1946].

Thus, when the acceptance of the norm is based upon the observable behaviour as it actually occurs in the society, then the validity is referred to the social *efficacy* of the norm, empirically verified, and the judges should apply the norm conscious of their binding force. Thus, a norm is valid law if and only if it is applied by the courts.

To answer the critics that a recently enacted statute does not yet offer elements to tell whether it will be or not followed by courts, Ross argued that the validity is an expression of the *probability* that the norm will be applied. A recently enacted norm is valid if and only if the previous behaviour of courts, their ideologies and the feelings on binding force reflects a high probability that the norm will be followed.

Note that the compliance with the norm may also vary in degree and dependent of various circumstances [Alexy, 1994, p.85-86], which makes the calculus for the probability of compliance a very difficult task. Quoting Alexy:

> The result is that the social efficacy of a norm and thereby its social validity is a matter of degree. A norm with a high degree of efficacy is complied with in, say, 80 per cent of the situations in which it is applicable, and a sanction is imposed in, say, 95 per cent of the cases of non-compliance. By contrast, the degree of efficacy is very low for a norm that is complied with in, say, merely 5 per cent of the situations in which it is applicable, and where a sanction is imposed in, say, merely 3 per cent of the cases of non-compliance. Between these extremes, however, the matter is less clear. Consider two norms, a norm at an 85 per cent level of compliance, but where a sanction is imposed in merely 1 per cent of the cases of non-compliance, and a norm at a mere 20 per cent level of compliance, but where a sanction is imposed in 98 per cent of the cases of non-compliance. The question of which of these two norms has a higher degree of social efficacy cannot be answered on the basis of the percentages alone. Any answer presupposes a determination, within the framework of the concept of social validity, of the relative significance of, on the one hand, compliance and, on the other, the imposition of a sanction for non-compliance.

Concepts of law primarily oriented toward issuance usually are the main concern of logical or conceptual analysis of the authorized agent's participation of settling the law. Issuance-oriented concepts of law are positivistic definitions of law. Hans Kelsen (in Kelsen [1960]) and Herbert L. A. Hart (in Hart [1958]) are the most significant representatives of this branch. The main difference upon the approaches of these two legal philosophers rests on the origin of the first norm that authorizes issuance. While in Hart's theory the law is a system of rule actually issued in accordance to a *rule of recognition* (which existence is a matter of fact), in Kelsen's theory the norms are issued in accordance to a presupposed *basic norm* (which is only imagined or thought).

In positivistic concepts of law, norms are altogether content-neutral, that is, it does not matter whether the content is ethical or not. The validity of a legal norm is established, thus, only by some formal requirements, having no relations with the values expressed by the norm. Therefore, the validity of the norm requires mainly two elements: the duly prescribed process and the duly authorized organ to enact the law (Kelsen [1960]).

Finally, in concepts of law primarily oriented toward the correctness of content, the validity of law is a moral validity, that is, the norm is valid law if it is *morally* justified. According to [Alexy, 1994, pp. 87]:

> An ethical concept of validity underlies the theories of natural law and the law of reason. The validity of a norm of natural law or a norm of the law of reason rests neither on its social efficacy nor on its authoritative issuance, but, rather, solely on the correctness of its content, to be demonstrated by moral justification.

Alexy addressed that a juridical validity demands the three elements altogether, that is, a norm is valid law if and only if it has authoritative issuance, social efficacy and correctness of content.

There exist other theories for the validity of the law. Several important works were proposed to explain the concept valid law, giving rise to numerous variations of sociological, positivistic and pragmatical theories. There are, among others, the following: the Theory of the Linguistic Rules of Recognition of Peczenik [1989], the Pure Theory of Law of Kelsen [1960], that are related to the theory of the rule of recognition of Hart [1961], the rational acceptability of the audience of Aarnio [1987], Aarnio *et al.* [1981], the chain of validity and the statements from a point of view of Raz [1975], the *boucles etranges* of Ost [1987], the theory of legal policies of Dworkin [1977], Dworkin [1967], the legal realism and the theory of normative ideology of judges of Ross [1946], the theory of Hägerström [1953], the actual acceptance of the legal community of Niiniluoto [1981], the theories of Rawls [1971], Vanquickenborne [1968], Olivecrona [1951] and several others. For a very complete survey see Tella [1998]. A very interesting approach to the validity of the law that deserves a mention, is the work of Moussallem [2001], based on the linguistic distinction of *enunciation-enunciated* and *enunciated-enunciated*, distinguishing between meta-language and object-language of duly enacted norms.

1.2.2.2 Defining Validity   Basically, we can say that the term "valid law" is mainly used with three meanings Aarnio *et al.* [1981] and Alexy [1994]: (i) it presupposes the existence of criteria of the law (authoritative *issuance*); (ii) it presupposes that the norm ought to be observed (social *efficacy*); and (iii) it presupposes a claim to be justifiable from the legal point of view (*correctness* of content). The last one does not mean a personal acceptance of the norm nor a definitive justification, but rather that profound reasons are expected in favour of the conclusion.

I shall start using the concept of valid law based upon syntactical and empirical elements, accepting the authoritative issuance and the social efficacy as necessary for settling the law. Then, I shall consider the underpinning reasons as a criterion of justification, aiming that the semantic level will be reached with the correctness of the content.

First of all, I shall define a legal norm[5] δ_i as valid law if and only if it belongs to some legal system $\Delta = \{\delta_1, \delta_2, ..., \delta_n\}$:

Definition 1 (Legal Norm) *A (normative) proposition δ_i is considered a legal norm with respect to a normative system Δ if and only if $\delta_i \in \Delta$.*

Obviously, this definition does not suffice *per se* to identify a valid legal norm δ_i, since it depends on the admissibility of δ_i on the respective normative system Δ. A legal norm δ_i must fulfill some criteria to be admissible in a legal system Δ (issuance), it also ought to be observed (efficacy) and should be morally justifiable (correctness).

In the next sections I shall define these elements.

1.2.2.3 Authoritative Issuance   I shall use in this work Kelsen's theory of the hierarchical structure of the law Kelsen [1960] to establish the criteria of admissibility of a legal norm in a legal system. According to Kelsen, the basis of validity of a legal norm is represented by another legal norm, such that the latter governs the process whereby the former is created. In the issuance level, the validity of norms, thus, is not given by its contents, i.e., human behavior specified by these norms. Recall that norms which are valid by virtue of their substance are the norms of morality. Legal norms instead have the content qualified by the content of a basic norm (Grundnorm) to which the issued norms can be traced back. Indeed, a norm is valid in the syntactical level if it was created in the way determined by another norm.

This represents a hierarchical ordering of various layers of legal norms, where the norm determining the creation of another norm is the higher-level norm, and the norm created in accordance with this determination is the lower-level norm. This yields a chain of validity whose regress leads to the ultimate basis of validity, that is, the Basic or Apex Norm (*Grundnorm*). Such hierarchical structure of the law is called *Stufenbau*, and it establishes a transitive and irreflexive ordering among legal norms, in the following order: Grundnorm, Constitution, General Norms (Statutes in civil law or precedents in common law), Individual Norms (administrative acts, individual judicial decisions, contract agreements) and the realization of coercive acts. This hierarchical structure of law is depicted in figure 1.1.

The Basic Norm (*Grundnorm*) is presupposed (Kelsen's earlier work) or a fiction (Kelsen's later work), that is, it is only imagined or thought, and the constitution is the highest level norm of positive law. Thus, the validity of lower-level norms is primarily oriented toward *issuance* according to a higher-level norm.

The constitution governs the organs and the process of general law creation: the duly prescribed process and the duly authorized organ. But the constitution also governs the *content* - though value-neutral - of future statutes. Usually, the content prescribed by constitution amounts only to a promise of statutes to be enacted, because it is not easy to attach a sanction to the failure to enact statutes having the

---

[5]Although been well aware about the distinction between *norm* and *normative proposition*, in this work I shall use the terms as synonymous. As long as the present work is concerned with the knowledge representation of the law and the derivability of legal consequences, the meaning of both expressions will be preserved, since the knowledge representation is based on the linguistic representation of the norm.

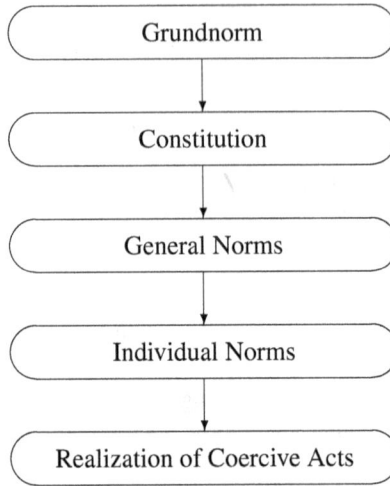

Figure 1.1   Kelsen's Hierarchical Structure of the Legal System (Stufenbau)

prescribed content. However, the constitution prevents the enactment of statutes of certain contents through the proscriptions of such statutes. This is used in the catalogue of civil rights and liberties, as the equality before law, the individual liberty, the freedom of conscience, and so forth. Since the content of a lower-level norm should be in accordance of the content of a higher-level norm, the unity of a legal system also requires the consistency between norms for the validity of legal norms. In other words, the content of a lower-level norm must be consistent with the content of a higher-level norm.

So, the authoritative issuance (legal validity) will be defined in this dissertation as the following:

Definition 2 (Authoritative Issuance) *A legal norm δ_i is authoritatively issued if and only if*

1. *$\Delta \cup \{\delta_i\}$ is consistent, that is, δ_i does not violate higher-ranking norms.*

2. *δ_i has been issued by an organ authorized by some $\delta_j \in \Delta$, for some $\delta_j \prec \delta_i$.*

3. *δ_i has been issued following the process established by some $\delta_j \in \Delta$, for some $\delta_j \prec \delta_i$.*

where $\prec$ is a transitive and irreflexive ordering (priority relation), established by the so-called Stufenbau.

The consistency criterion in issuance is controversial. A lower-level norm may not be consistent or can establish an exception for the application of a higher-level norm, whenever the former does not exclude an essential property of the latter. This feature is in the core of nonmonotonic reasoning and will be discussed in detail in the next sections.

Moreover, as long as the consistency is regarded to the content of a norm - though its ethical-neutral content -, one might argue that consistency is not necessary and a norm is valid if it is duly enacted. Actually, legal validity (issuance) presupposes that only the formal criteria need to be fulfilled. For instance, when the content of the inferior legal norm conflicts with the content of a superior legal norm (for example, the Constitution), the problem does not stand at the issuance level (the inferior norm was enacted in a duly prescribed process and by a duly authorized organ). In this case, the legal norm keeps its (legal) validity, since the criteria defined by Kelsen [1960] to be valid are primarily formal and were fulfilled. Therefore, according to some authors, the consistency criterion is not essential to define validity. The consistency problem is then regarded by the literature as a efficacy problem.

1.2.2.4 Social Efficacy Actually, Kelsen accepts that the *efficacy* is a necessary element for the validity of norms Kelsen [1960]. In this work, the efficacy of legal norms is regarded with the compliance to the norm or the imposition of a sanction in the case of non-compliance Alexy [1994]. If the lower-level norm is not consistent with a higher-level norm and there exists no sanction for the inconsistency (for instance, by considering the lower-level norm as invalid law), then the higher-level norm is inefficacious.

Let us take the following example to illustrate it. As we have seen, a legal rule enacted by the legislative branch is binding, that is, it ought to be observed. In Brazilian law, for example, the criminal statute notice adultery as a criminal offense. However, the Brazilian courts no longer apply such rule. They claim that adultery still is immoral and has civil consequences, but can non longer justify a criminal charge. So, the criminal statute (general norm) was reversed by case decision (individual norm), which has a lower level than the former. In this case, the criminal statute is a valid norm and is also binding (or at least it should be), but it is inefficacious. When a legal norm is inefficacious over a certain period, it is said that it loses its validity (*desuetudo*).

In [Aarnio *et al.*, 1981, pp. 143], the *Grundnorm* differs from the concept given by Kelsen in two ways: (i) the *Grundnorm* is conditioned by a if-then clause with three conditions: (a) some facts and/or values, (b) the legal point of view; (c) the underpinning reasons, whether they are placed within the if-then clause or as an external condition; and (ii) in Kelsen's theory, the "efficacy" of the legal order is an external condition, while in Aarnio *et al.* [1981]'s theory it is one of many facts to which the if-then clause might refer.

The realism Ross [1946] attempted to overcoming the dualism of validity and efficacy treating the problem as validity and reality, that is, the probability of applying the law by the courts.

Hence, as a necessary element to the validity of law, the efficacy of legal norms must be defined:

Definition 3 (Social Efficacy) *Alexy [1994] A legal norm δ_i is socially efficacious if and only if the observable behaviour is complied with δ_i or a sanction is imposed for non-compliance.*

The consistency of a legal system, then, is directly related to the efficacy of legal norms. A lower-level norm can be authoritatively issued, in spite of the non-compliance with a higher-level norm and the failure in imposing a sanction[6].In this case, the higher-level norm is not regarded as efficacious, and the problem of consistency can be considered solved. But we cannot completely ignore the consistency, leaving the problem to the efficacy level alone. Here is where there is a relationship between efficacy and issuance. A legal system must be consistent, avoiding contradictory obligations. Therefore, the efficacy element also implies a consistency check for legal systems.

Efficacy is a necessary element for the validity of law, as well as consistency. However, the notion of consistency given in classical logics does not tolerate conflicting information. Hence, the consistency required on item 1 of definition 2 will be extended in Chapter 3, Section 3.3.5 to accept conflicting information.

The distinction between issuance (legal validity) and efficacy (social validity) in this work is justified by the following: issuance is a feature that a certain behaviour *ought* (*Sollen*) to be observed, while efficacy is a feature that a behaviour *is* (*Sein*) observed or a sanction *is* imposed. The former belongs to the ideal set of legal norms, and the latter belongs to how the world actually is (observable behaviour). So, it is necessary to keep the dualism issuance-efficacy to handle separately both the is-ought problem (*Sollen*) and the ought-is problem (*Sein*).

This is one of the most important and, at the same time, the most hardest to solve problems in legal theory: the connection between the linguistic level (legal norms) and the empirical level (the world as it actually is). One thus has two main problems to solve in legal reasoning: (i) the *is-ought* problem (issuance level), that is, transforming social facts in law; and (ii) the *ought-is* problem (efficacy level), i.e., verifying whether the law is actually obeyed (social facts generated by law). Recall that some authors Kelsen [1960] Aarnio *et al.* [1981] put the efficacy problem inside the validity level. This is a quite attractive approach, because one should not even imagine accepting a valid law which is not applicable. A valid law is not only allegorical.

Actually, legal systems do need a tool to make the law observed, that is, to make legal norms efficacious. Quoting Bedaque, in his remarkable book Bedaque [2001], *"... one also cannot conceive the substantive law without a tool to make it efficacious"*. Usually, such tools are usually established by substantive sanctions and by procedural rules (coercive acts), which is also enacted through authoritative issuance.

1.2.2.5 *Binding Norms*   One may think that an inefficacious norm is not binding. Otherwise, it should be applied from a legal point of view. At first glance, and in

---

[6]Usually, the sanction for inconsistency (non-compliance of the lower-level norm with the higher-level norm) is the invalidity of the lower-level norm.

a naive definition, a legal norm is said to be efficacious (in force) if it ought to be observed from the legal point of view. But, what does it mean that a norm *"ought to be observed"*? Some authors claim that a norm ought to be observed from a legal point of view, if the norm is binding. Then, one could think that a legal norm is efficacious if and only if it is binding.

However, such assertion is not quite accurate. It may happen that a binding norm should not be applied in an individual case, showing its lack of efficacy. For instance, when an exception clause is built to exclude the consequent of the norm, one may have a binding norm, which will not be efficacious, since the behavior was not in compliance with the norm and a sanction is not imposed for non-compliance.

Therefore, a legal norm may not lose its binding feature in the presence of an exception clause. A norm is binding iff it ought to be observed (*Sollen*) from the legal point of view; and it is efficacious iff it is actually observed (*Sein*) from the social point of view (social facts).

Following Peczenik [1989], the *"binding"* feature of a legal norm δ_i will be kept, be it a statutory rule (civil law) or a judicial precedent (common law), by requiring its use in the justification of another legal norm (viz. a judicial decision), as a reason or as a counter-reason, i.e., it must be in the legal knowledge base Δ when some legal norm is inferred.

Definition 4 (Binding Norm) *Peczenik [1989] A legal norm δ_i is binding if and only if δ_i is necessarily used in the justification of ψ, that is, iff $\delta_i \in \Delta$ whenever $\Delta \mid\!\sim \psi$.*

With these elements, the definition of validity can be revised.

1.2.2.6 Validity Revisited Now, we can define a criterion of admissibility criterion for legal norms to reach only those norms that are produced in accordance with the determination of a higher-level norm, in a duly prescribed way and by a duly authorized organ (issuance), and where either the social behaviour is complied with or a sanction is imposed (efficacy).

Definition 5 *A legal norm δ_i is admissible with respect to Δ if and only if δ_i is authoritatively issued and socially efficacious.*

Next, I shall extend the definition of validity given by Definition 1 in the following:

Definition 6 *[Validity] A legal norm δ_i is valid law if and only if δ_i is admissible with respect to Δ.*

But it does not suffice to define validity, since it is necessary to establish the (correct) content of legal norms, to prevent lawlessness law (*unrecht*).

1.2.2.7 Correctness of Content The discussion in the literature about the connection or the separation of law and moral is very intense. I shall not intend to bring the discussion to this dissertation, just accepting one of the theses. As long as the legal theory adopted in this work is mainly based on Alexy's approach, it will be to accept the connection thesis. Alexy's theory is based on Radbruch's formula of extreme injustice. Quoting Radbruch [1946], *apud* Alexy [1994]:

> The conflict between justice and legal certainty may well be resolved in this way: The positive law, secured by legislation and power, takes precedence even when its content is unjust and inexpedient, unless the conflict between statute and justice reaches such an intolerable degree that the statute, as 'lawless law', must yield to justice.

Notice that Radbruch does not deny the legal character of an unjust norm. To him, such is forfeited only when there exists an *"intolerable degree"* of injustice.

Usually, the literature regards the correctness of content of legal norms as a pragmatical problem, that is, such is a relation of the norm with the interpreter (personal acceptance). This approach is very subjective and thus must be avoided from a scientific point of view. An authorized organ (like the judge) may do not recognize a valid norm as binding or say that, although supposed binding, it has not to be observed. But one could ask which organ is legitimated to recognize a valid norm as binding.

There is a distinction originated from H.L.A. Hart, between internal and external points of view, which Alexy calls the participant and the observer's perspective. According to Alexy [1994], at the observer's perspective one will not ask whether the decision is correct or not, but, rather, how decisions are actually made. From the participant's perspective some arguments are adduced for or against certain contents, showing how a case would be decided to be correctly. Quoting [Alexy, 1994, pp. 25]:

> At the centre of the participant's perspective stands the judge. When other participants - say, legal scholars, attorneys, or interested citizens - adduce arguments for or against certain contents of the legal system, they refer in the end to how a judge would have do decide if he wanted to decide correctly.

Thus, when deciding for the application of a legal norm - at the participant's perspective -, the authorized organ usually considers the reasons for and the reasons against the acceptance of that legal norm with respect to a certain legal system. This can be defined in the following:

Definition 7 *[Acceptable Legal Norm] A legal norm δ_i is acceptable with respect to a normative system Δ iff*

1. there exists no argument δ_j against δ_i, for all $\delta_i \in \Delta$.

2. the argument δ_j against δ_i is outweighed by Δ.

An argument δ_j is outweighed by Δ if and only if δ_j is outweighed either by δ_i which it attacks or by some δ_k, for all $\{\delta_i, \delta_j, \delta_k\} \in \Delta$.

Now we are ready to define the correctness of the content of legal norms:

Definition 8 *[Correctness of Content] A legal norm δ_i is ethically valid iff δ_i is acceptable with respect to Δ.*

The three elements of the concept and validity of law, as identified by Alexy (authoritative issuance, social efficacy and correctness of content), yield a sound and complete legal theory. Both legal and social validity (issuance and efficacy) are concerned only with the ideal level, that is, with the syntactical level of the theory. Hence, δ_i is valid norm with respect to Δ iff $\Delta \vdash \delta_i$. The ethical validity (correctness) is related to which behaviour in the content of the norm is correct, i.e., with the semantical level of the theory. So, δ_i is correct with respect to Δ iff $\Delta \vDash \delta_i$.

We say that a legal theory is *sound* iff every legal norm provable from the legal system Δ is entailed by the legal system, or if $\Delta \vdash \delta$ then $\Delta \vDash \delta$; and a legal theory is *complete* iff every legal norm entailed by the legal system is provable from the legal system, or if $\Delta \vDash \delta$ then $\Delta \vdash \delta$. In a word, a legal theory is *sound* iff every issued and efficacious norm is content correct, and it is *complete* iff every content correct norm is issued and efficacious norm. Therefore, we should look for a logical model for legal reasoning that sanctions issuance, efficacy and correctness of legal norms.

One should be aware that the term *complete* used here does not mean the *completeness* of legal systems, in the sense of inexistence of gaps in law. Rather, the legal system is full of gaps, as was demonstrated by Bulygin [2003] in a very impressive work. This feature also justifies the necessity of including value statements and moral principles within the legal system Δ.

Since the definition of correctness of content of legal norms is based on reasons included in a legal system Δ, we must specify which arguments can be considered in Δ.

1.2.3   Including Arguments in a Legal System

Some relevant reasons $\varphi_1, ..., \varphi_n$ may form an argument for or against an outcome ψ, if these reasons put forward a claim for our belief. This assertion puts in relief the conditional structure of an argument, $\varphi_1, ..., \varphi_n \rightarrow \psi$, although not all conditionals are arguments Copi [1961]. If the argument is based in law, then it will be a normative argument. Hereinafter, the argument is thought of as it is in object level, if the language is expressive enough for this account. Notice that if the argument has no antecedent, then we should consider the antecedent as a logical truth.

Basically, the arguments are mainly formed by rules (civil law systems) or by precedents (common law systems), as long as they are binding. However, an argument may also include principles, legal goals and legal values within its premises. Remark that, according to some authors, moral principles, non-legal values and goals that are not recognized by the members of a legal community cannot support a legal outcome and thus, cannot belong to a legal system. See Hage [1997] for a detailed discussion.

Moreover, the *uncertainty* of legal norms is usually regarded as a natural feature of legal reasoning. One may think on the uncertainty as the "open texture" Hart [1958] or the "fuzziness" Peczenik and Wróblewski [1985] of legal norms. Recall the well-known paper from [Hart, 1958, p.22] distinguishing "clear" ("core") cases from "hard" ("penumbra") cases. According to Peczenik [1989], in "clear" cases, the decision follows from a set containing only a legal rule, a description of the facts and perhaps some other premises which can be easily proved. In "hard" cases, however, the decision follows from an expanded set of premises containing a value statement, moral principles, goals and statements which are not easy to prove. Even a detailed higher-level norm which meticulously establishes the contents of lower-level norm, leaves a number of determinations to the latter carrying it out. The organ authorized to enact the lower-level norm must use its own discretion to fill in the command, since the higher-level norm has not foreseen and, for the most part, cannot foresee the entire set of premises. Thus, moral principles cannot be excluded from a legal knowledge base.

Rules generate arguments that should be included in Δ, and some authors claim that rules can be weighed too (cf. [Peczenik, 1989, pp. 80 ff.] and [Verheij, 1996, pp.48 ff.]. Usually, moral principles are replaced in law by rules, which restrict the need for weighing reasons. However, legal rules have also a *prima-facie* character (see Section 1.3.1 forthcoming), and often are weighed against counter-arguments, even when these counter-arguments are based on principles.

Obviously, the facts are reasons too (or according to Hage [1997], the real reasons), and must be included on Δ. Notice that even indirect evidence can strengthen the belief in a conclusion.

A principle or a value can be a *prima-facie* reason for action [Peczenik, 1989, pp. 75]. Hence, such can be a relevant reason to warrant a claim and to be weighed against other reasons. After [Alexy, 1985, pp. 76] and [Peczenik, 1989, pp. 75 ff.], a *value* is defined as a criterion of evaluation, i.e., as a certain ideal. A *principle* establishes such an ideal (in other words, a value), which can be carried into effect to a certain degree. Thus, a principle establishes what is *prima-facie* obligatory, while a value shows what is *prima-facie*, at best.

Goals have also an essential role in legal reasoning (McCormick [1978], Summers [1978]). Examples of goals that received widespread support in law are human rights Alexy [1985]. A goal generates reasons for acting in order to achieve that goal. Legal values and principles represent a kind of goal, though there are differences between them, as was pointed out by [Hage, 1997, pp. 99].

Hence, several relevant circumstances may form an argument or a reason for or against a conclusion.

A legal system[7] Δ is a collection of legal norms $\delta_i : \phi \rightarrow \psi$, which represent legal rules, precedents, principles, values or goals. Principles, values or goals do not have antecedent, and is denoted by $\delta_i : \top \rightarrow \psi$, since they are unconditional ideals.

1.3   Uncertainty in Law

Another feature that characterizes legal systems is its uncertainty. A higher-level norm which governs the creation of a lower-level norm, will never foresee every detail in the prescription of a state of affairs. There will always be a range of discre-

---

[7]In this work I do not distinguish between legal system and legal knowledge base.

tion, either wider or narrower, and there also always remains an existence of possible exception not noticed by the law. This will be discussed in the next Section.

1.3.1   Prima-Facie and All-Things-Considered Obligations

The literature distinguishes between *prima-facie* obligations and *all-things-considered* obligations ([Ross, 1930, pp. 28], [Hintikka, 1971, pp. 91 ff.], [Alchourrón, 1993, pp. 65 ff.] and others).

Usually, our culture compels us to endorse moral judgements only when they are definitive statements Peczenik [1989]. A normative argument is *definitive* if one no longer pays attention to reasons against the conclusion Peczenik [1989]. Otherwise, the argument is only *prima-facie*. According to Ross [1930], an obligation is *prima-facie* on the basis of an underlying principle, if the act tends to be a 'duty proper', though the act itself may also be invalidated in some circumstances. For instance, a statement that a thief ought to be punished is a rule with a *prima-facie* character, since in some circumstances it can be invalidated, as when the thief is a minor.

Prima-facie obligations thus, can generate defeasible[8] arguments, that is, arguments for conclusions that can be overridden. Remark that defeasible arguments are the main concerns of the non-monotonic reasoning, a subfield of Artificial Intelligence.

By comparing all *prima-facie* obligations and all relevant circumstances, one can yield an all-things-considered outcome.

According to Peczenik [1989], an obligation has (i) the all-things-considered quality *senso stricto* if and only if it has considerations regarding all morally relevant circumstances and all criteria of coherent reasoning, and (ii) the all-things-considered quality *senso largo* if and only if it has support of as many morally relevant circumstances as possible and as many criteria of coherent reasoning as possible. A question addressed by the literature Sieckmann [2003] is whether prima-facie statements can yield definitive all-things-considered statements, usually answering that it is not possible. To answer this question, first we must answer whether there exists in law definitive all-things-considered obligations. Peczenik explains that *"no human being has resources sufficient to formulate all-things-considered statements sensu stricto"* [Peczenik, 1989, pp. 76]. Hence, he emphasizes the all-things-considered quality *senso largo*, in what he calls *ceteris paribus* all-things-considered statements.

A *ceteris paribus* all-things-considered argument demands that as many relevant circumstances as possible are taken into consideration in weighing and balancing[9]. This is a quite frequent process in law, and it also suggests that, in this subject matter, there are not many normative arguments (whether there exists one...) which are definitive by themselves, but rather that they must be weighed against other circumstances that are contrary to the conclusion. In law, for example, there are some

---

[8]The origin of the term 'defeasible' is credited to Hart [1949], although it was originally applied to concepts instead of arguments. However, there are older references to the word 'defeasible'.
[9]After Peczenik [1989], the term *ceteris paribus* is used in this work as equivalent to *as many ... as possible*.

procedural restrictions to be applied over the argumentation of the plaintiff or the defendant. These restrictions aim at making the weighing process a finite one. Obviously, the law cannot extend indefinitely the opportunity of the parties to address their reasons. In some legal systems, for instance, the circumstances to be weighed are the reasons that arise from the relief sought and the facts adduced in support of that demand, and no other reason can be added by the plaintiff in the course of the demand.

In other systems, the judgement includes in *res judicata* the totality of the underlying reasons, regardless of whether they were addressed in the particular proceeding or not. But this does not mean that an all-things-considered statement *senso stricto* was produced. Even a final decision (*res judicata*) does not keep within an absolute value of immutability. One cannot expect an all-things-considered statement *senso stricto* even when the underlying reasons that were not argued, have *merged* with the judgement, with the result that the plaintiff cannot sue anew by virtue of *res judicata*. In the words of Mary Kay Kane [Kane, 1993, pp.225]:

> There are some circumstances in which even though the standard for applying res judicata has been met, preclusion will not result. These situations arise when the judicial economy policies fostered by claim preclusion are outweighed by some other public policy underlying the type of action that is envolved.

According to Currie, *apud* Dinamarco [2003]:

> Courts can only do their best to determine the truth on the basis of the evidence, and the first lesson one must learn on the subject of res judicata is that judicial findings must not be confused with absolute truth.

Therefore, although a binding norm (valid law) is used in the justification of judicial decisions, it can be overruled by another norm or reason that has priority over it. For the purpose of this research, we thus need a logical system that allows the inference over defeasible norms, that is, allowing a consequence relation generated by "jumping" over unknown premises. For such account, we should emphasize the theory of Peczenik [1989].

1.3.2   The Theory of Transformation in Law

The theory of transformation in law was developed by Alexander Peczenik Peczenik [1989], Aarnio *et al.* [1981], and I shall use it with some slight modification. The theory detaches from the fact that all justified evaluations are based on transformations, i.e., on *jumps* from one layer to another. The inference in law is not different, and usually demands a transformation, that is, a jump. Quoting Peczenik in Aarnio *et al.* [1981], *'like any knowledge, the knowledge of the law depends on "jumps"'*. A transformation is defined as follows:

Definition 9 *[Aarnio et al., 1981, pp. 137] A transformation is performed if and only if ϕ is brought forward as a reason for ψ, and ϕ does not deductively entail ψ.*

A transformation is represented in Aarnio *et al.* [1981] by $\phi \top \psi$. In this dissertation however, I shall denote a transformation by $\phi \mathbin{\vert\!\sim} \psi$, that is, a defeasible jump to a legal consequence in the absence of reasons against it. Thus, I shall use the operator $\mid\sim$ suggested by Gabbay, as will be discussed in section 2.2.1 of Chapter 2. As noticed in the underlying legal theory, naturally the propositions ϕ and ψ may have more propositions resulting in a more complex formula $\phi_1, ..., \phi_m \mid\sim \psi_1, ..., \psi_n$.

In the context of justification, i.e., whether knowledge produced by *jumps* is justified or not, legal norms can be attacked of defended. This suggests that jumpings should be regulated by rules, that is, by transformation rules. A rule R_i^t is a transformation rule if and only if $R_i^t \cup \{\phi\}$ logically entail ψ. After Aarnio *et al.* [1981], I shall distinguish between three different cases concerning transformation rules: (i) cases in which jumps hold from transformation rules; (ii) cases in which transformation rules are interpreted, restricted, extended or abandoned; (iii) cases to which there is no transformation rule.

Notice that Aarnio *et al.* [1981] accepts a "transformation" of facts, non-legal values and non-legal norms into the law, in what they call *category-transformation* and *criteria-transformation*. Such transformations are actually *jumping* from 'is' (*Sein*) to 'ought' (*Sollen*). They claim that by such jumps *"the move into the realm of the law is accomplished"* [Alexy, 1994, pp. 105]. For a deep understanding of this elegant theory, see Aarnio *et al.* [1981]. However, I shall not make this assumption in this work, since the 'is' and the 'ought' belongs to categories that are of altogether different kinds, and such a "jump"can lead to the *is-ought* problem and the *Naturalistic Fallacy* pointed out by Hume and Moore, respectively. Thus, from an 'is' we cannot derive an 'ought' and vice-versa. For an attempt to overcome this problem, the interested reader should see Correas [1995], which suggests an impressive theory based on a social-semiological approach to justify such 'jumps', and also the remarkable work of Wróblewski [1981] and Wróblewski [1988].

In a more recent work Peczenik [1989], Peczenik refined the concept of transformation, defining it in the following:

Definition 10 *[Peczenik, 1989, pp.116] [Transformation Revisited] A step from a set of premises Δ to a conclusion ψ is a transformation iff Δ does not deductively entail ψ and Δ cannot be expanded in such a way that Δ_i occurs with the following conditions:*

1. Δ_i deductively entails ψ

2. Δ_i consists solely of certain premises, proved premises, and premises presupposed in the considered culture

Notice that the definition of Transformation excludes logical deduction. The reason seems to be quite obvious: If there is a logical deduction (in the sense of classical logic) then certainly there is not a jump. The condition 2 prevents Δ from been formed only by strict conditionals. Otherwise, the conclusion will be deduced from non-contestable premises, that is, there will be a logical deduction (in classical logic sense). I shall not discuss about certain, proved and presupposed premises to not deviate from the scope of this work. The interested reader should see Peczenik [1989].

Remark that the definition allows the expansion of the set of premises Δ with non-certain premises. Nevertheless, as long as we add non-certain premises, i.e., premises that are not analyctically true, we could have any kind of jump. This feature, however, is not completely desirable, since it can lead to unreasonable conclusions. Thus, the definition of a transformation should be constrained to admit only reasonable jumps.

Definition 11 *[Peczenik, 1989, pp. 117, 131] [Reasonable Transformation] A transformation from Δ to ψ is reasonable iff the transformation can be converted into a deductivelly correct inference through adding some new premises to Δ, creating a finite and logically consistent set of premises containing:*

1. some old premisses ϕ_i that already belong to Δ

2. new reasonable premisses ϕ_j, $i < j \leq n$, where n is finite

The addition of premises in the reasoning chain actually detaches the *enthymematic* feature of legal reasoning, as was pointed out by Adeodato [1999]. So, it is very common to draw a conclusion in legal reasoning without a premiss that allows a deductively correct inference. However, as long as any consciousness content only exists if and only if it is converted into a discourse, i.e., it is formalized in a language (see section 1.2.3), the missing premiss should be formalized in a discourse (language) and added to the set of premises Δ, despite the enthymematic feature of legal reasoning.

The added premiss must be reasonable, to avoid arbitrary conclusions. This makes the reasonable jump dependent of the definition of what is considered a reasonable premiss, which are defined as follows:

Definition 12 *[Peczenik, 1989, pp. 131] [Reasonable Premisses] A premiss ϕ_i is reasonable iff*

1. ϕ_i is not falsified

2. it is not the case that ϕ_i does not logically follow from a highly coherent set of premisses

Despite the concept of reasonableness being very difficult to define, as noticed by Peczenik [1989], a premiss ϕ_i can be considered reasonable if it is neither falsified nor arbitrary. In other words, a premiss ϕ_i is as more reasonable as more attempts to falsify it fail, and also if it is not *evidently improbable* that the premiss ϕ_i follows from a highly coherent set of statements Peczenik [1989].

◼ EXAMPLE 1.3

[Reasonable Jump] [Peczenik, 1989, pp. 116] Consider the following steps from premisses ϕ_i in Δ to a conclusion ψ, denoted by $\Delta \hspace{-0.5em}\sim \psi$:

$$\Delta = \left\{ \begin{array}{l} \phi_1 : \neg hm \\ \phi_2 : hp \\ \phi_3 : \neg hm \land hp \to gp \end{array} \right\} \over \psi : gp$$ (1.1)

Conditionals ϕ_i and ψ represent the following situations: [ϕ_1] John Doe normally does not harm others ($\neg hm$), and [ϕ_2] normally helps (hp) others. [ϕ_3] If a person does not harm others and helps others, then normally he is a good person (gp). [ψ] John Doe is a good person.

One can easily see that ϕ_3 is not analytically true, and also that ϕ_3 is neither falsified nor arbitrary, i.e., it is not the case that ϕ_3 does not follow from a highly coherent set of premises. Thus, there is certainly a transformation (jump) and a reasonable one.

Consider now a set Δ', without the premiss ϕ_3. According to definition 11, the set Δ' can be expanded to include ϕ_3 and, thus, ψ still is the result of a transformation.

However, if one regards ϕ_3 as analytically true, then the step from ϕ_1 and ϕ_2 to the conclusion ψ, whether ϕ_3 was originally in Δ or not, is not a transformation, because the jump can be converted into logical deduction based on premises analytically true, i.e., all premises would be *certain*.

It should be emphasized that in example 1.3, ϕ_3 is not a *certain* premiss. The moral judgement made to formulate ϕ_3 had considered only some moral criteria ignoring others such as the disposition to work, telling the truth, showing courage, etc. Therefore, based on example 1.3, John Doe would be regarded by jump as a good person, even if he had been a lazy and a liar coward (cf. [Peczenik, 1989, pp. 115]).

This suggests that a reasonable premiss is either a highly probable defeasible conditional or a strict conditional added to a conditional knowledge base Δ with defeasible conditionals in the reasoning chain.

Since this work is oriented to model legal reasoning, the conditional knowledge base Δ should be formed by legal norms. Legal norms are thus premises that support a transformation.

1.3.3 The Concept of Coherence

As long as the definitions of *reasonable jump* (Definition 11) and *reasonable premisses* (Definition 12) are highly dependent of the definition of coherence, a word should be given about this issue. The following was extracted from Peczenik [1989] and is briefly described here just as a reference, since it will not be analysed in the present work. I believe that the final translation will entail coherent jumps in a higher degree, but this result was not investigated in this work.

According to Peczenik [1989], coherence is better understood as extensive (numerous and long chains of justification) and general statements. Coherence is a matter of degree. Thus, a theory is as more coherent as more the statements belonging to a given theory approximate a perfect supportive structure. A supportive structure is formed by the minimum condition of coherence (that is, the existence of statements supported by reasons) and by 10 criteria and principles of coherence Peczenik [1989]. The interested reader should see [Peczenik, 1989, pp. 161 ff.]. Next, I shall briefly enumerate the 10 principles of coherence as they are formulated by Peczenik.

1. THE NUMBER OF SUPPORTIVE RELATIONS

   One should justify as many statements as possible.

2. THE LENGTH OF THE SUPPORTIVE CHAINS

   When justifying a statement, one should support it with as long a chain of reasons as possible, such that p_1 supports p_2, p_2 supports p_3 and so on.

3. STRONG SUPPORT

   One should formulate statements which are strongly justified by as many statements as possible.

4. CONNECTION BETWEEN SUPPORTIVE CHAINS

   When justifying a statement, one should formulate premises supporting as many different conclusions as possible, and as many independent sets of premisses (cumulation of reasons) supporting it as possible.

5. PRIORITY ORDERS BETWEEN REASONS

   When one faces a collision of principles used as premises which justify a statement, one should formulate as many priority relations between them as possible.

6. RECIPROCAL JUSTIFICATION

   When using a theory to justify a statement, one should expect that the theory covers as many reciprocal empirical relations, analytic relations and normative relations between statements belonging it as possible.

7. GENERALITY OF CONCEPTS

   When using a theory to justify a statement, one should see to it that the theory is expressed in as many general concepts and in as highly general concepts as possible, and also one should make as complete a list as possible of the resemblances between the concepts belonging to the theory.

8. CONCEPTUAL CROSS-CONNECTIONS

   When using a theory to justify a statement, one should express it in as many concepts similar to those used in other theories as possible.

9. NUMBER OF CASES

   A theory used to justify a statement should cover as many individual cases as possible.

10. DIVERSITY OF FIELDS OF LIFE

A theory used to justify a statement should conver as many fields of life as possible.

As long as the coherence is measured in degrees, and since the principles of coherence should not be taken in isolation from others, the degree of coherence is determined by weighing and balancing Peczenik [1989]. The higher the degree, the more coherent the theory.

1.4   Priority between Normative Propositions

Up to this point, some legal norms are considered admissible in a legal system. Nevertheless, it was not specified which norm has priority over another one when two norms are incompatible. Thus, a criterion of preference between normative propositions is essential to establish priorities in the case of a clash of normative propositions.

This problem claims for two distinct approaches. The first one is based on meta-rules to solve the problem of conflicting legal norms, as defended in the literature. However, there exist situations when such criteria cannot be used, because either there are no priority relations, as in the case of collision of principles, or when legal norms have only indirect evidence for its conclusion. This problem usually requires balancing among incompatible outcomes. In Section 1.4.1 I shall discuss the priority relation based on meta-rules, and in Section 1.4.2 the problem of weighing and balancing will be introduced.

1.4.1   Meta-rules for the Conflict between Norms

Usually, legal systems provide meta-rules to solve the problem of incompatible legal norms, whether they are explicitly enacted or not. For a very complete analysis of these features, see Bobbio [1982]. There are three basic rules to solve the problem of conflict between legal rules: Temporal, hierarchical and specificity criteria.

The temporal criterion gives priority to a more recently enacted norm, that is, the later rule has precedence over the earlier one. It is the so-called *Lex Posterior derogat Priori* principle. According to such principle, in the case of rules enacted by the same authority, the last one in time should prevail.

The hierarchical criterion is based on the Kelsen's theory of hierarchical structure of the law (*Stufenbau*), gives preference to those norms that belong to a higher stratum in this structure instead of those belonging to lower-level strata. For instance, a constitutional norm should prevail over ordinary statutes. This principle is also known as *Lex Superior derogat inferiori*.

The last criterion reflects the specificity principle (*Lex specialis derogat generali*), such that a rule has priority over another rule if the former is more specific than the latter.

Based on these three principles, one has a meta-norm to solve the priority problem between norms. The main problem arises when these criteria conflict with each

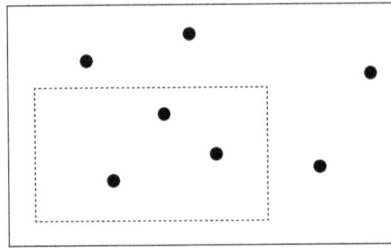

Figure 1.2   Frame generated by a higher norm

other. For instance, a later rule which should have precedence (based on *Lex Posterior* principle), may be more general than the earlier rule which, according to the specificity principle (*Lex Specialis*), should also prevail. So, which rule has priority? The later one? Or the more specific one? This phenomenon also occurs between the temporal principle and the hierarchical principle (when a later rule has lower hierarch than the earlier one), and between the specificity and the hierarchical principles (when a more specific rule has a lower hierarch than a higher-level more general one).

To solve the conflict between the meta-rules, the literature usually regards the temporal principle as a *weak* criterion, and the hierarchical and the specificity principles as *strong* criteria (for all, see Bobbio [1982]). Thus, in the case of a conflict between the temporal (*weak*) and the hierarchical principle (*strong* criterion), the latter should prevail. In the same sense, when there is a conflict between the temporal (*weak*) and the specificity (*strong*) principles, the specificity criterion should have priority. However, there may be a conflict between two strong principles. In this case, no solution is given by the literatute at all.

Some authors have advocated that the hierarchical principle should always prevail. However, I claim that in general case, the specificity principle must prevail, giving priority to more exceptional rules over general ones, even when the former are lower-level norms and the latter higher-level ones. The hierarchical principle should prevail only when the more specific rule dismisses an essential property of the general rule. It may look surprising that a more specific lower-level rule has priority over a more general higher-level rule. However, it happens because the higher-level norm cannot predict any detail to be accomplished in by way of the act. The relation between higher-level and lower-level (e.g., constitution and statutes, statutes and judicial decisions, and so forth) norms can be pictured as a frame (viz. Kelsen [1934]) within which various possibilities for application are given. Thus, each element of this frame is a possible act to be applied. The frame given by a higher-level norm is depicted in Figure 1.2, where the frame box means a higher-level norm and a dash box means a lower-level norm. As one can easily see, a lower-level norm can choose some elements (interpretations) excluding others. This normally happens because a lower-level norm is usually more specific, considering some circumstances that are relevant to a subset of individuals but irrelevant for characterize the whole set. I wish to emphasize that the frame I made used to explain the specificity relation does not imply my personal acceptance of Kelsen's theory of interpretation. The frame was used only to illustrate the possibility of exceptions in law, based on the assumption that a higher-level norm cannot foresee the contents of a lower-level one, which can be more specific.

1.4.2 Weighing and Balancing

Whereas the meta-rules for the conflict of norms are mainly directed to statutes (legal rules), there may exist collision between principles, goals and values. Such cannot be solved by colision rules, since one does not have specificity, hierarchy or temporal relations between them. Notice also, that legal interpretation of statutes (for instance an interpretation respecting the intentions of the legislative branch, or one oriented to a socially desirable result), may claim for another method of given priority to legal norms. In such cases, we may have to weigh and balance reasons.

According to [Hage, 1997, pp. 124], the process of weighing and balancing is a metaphor. It suggests that a set of zero or more reasons for a state of affairs outweighs a set of zero or more reasons against that state of affairs. In this metaphor, each set of reasons is mentally placed on the scale of a balance, and the "heavier" (most acceptable) set outweighs the other one. To quote Hage:

> In fact there are no such balances which can help weighing reasons. There will be a mental process that leads to a certain outcome in the case that we have both reasons for and reasons against a particular outcome.

Although this mental process, whether unconscious or not, may not necessarily provide a rationale for the acceptance of a set of reasons, I shall only discuss in this work the case where we do have reasons why one set outweighs the other one. This approach is based on an assumption that we only have a rational decision if we have reasons why such a decision should prevail, and these reasons are not outweighed. This does not mean, however, that a decision is only rational if we have reasons for it. Instead, this means that if we are able to give reasons for a decision, and the reasons against it are outweighed, then the decision can be viewed as rational[10].

Two main issues that point out to balancing are the clash of reasons and the disregard of irrelevant reasons. Since weighing deals with inconsistent information, naturally it yields a clash of reasons (reasons for and reasons against a state of affairs). Such process also should be able to ignore irrelevant reasons, that is, reasons which cannot change the weight of the arguments. These are the two main properties that characterize balancing.

Nevertheless, these features do not suffice for the task of weighing. Actually, there is one more property that is necessary for the weighing process. In many cases, reasons which individually are outweighed by other reasons, together *'weigh'* more

---

[10]Notice that such a problem goes far beyond this assumption. Prof. Oscar Correas Correas [1995], for instance, investigated the socio-semiological structure of law, claiming that, typically, the "real" reasons of the law (capitalism described by Marxist theory) are hidden within the discourse of law, while the reasons actually used are not what motivate the law at all.

than the reason which initially was stronger (cf. Hage [1997], Verheij [1996]). Explaining this phenomenon in weighing, Peczenik writes [Peczenik, 1997a, pp. 1-2]:

> Thus, weighing can be conceptualized aggregation of arguments and construction of chains of arguments. As soon as one states that one thing weighs more than another, the question occurs "Why?" Then, one needs another argument and another act of weighing. Briefly: x may weigh more than y in isolation but, in a certain situation, z can occur, and reverse the order: x weighs less than y+z. In this way, the weights can be aggregated (cf. Peczenik [1997b]).
>
> To be sure, not all reasons may be cumulated. But reasons proffered in legal argumentation cumulate often enough to make cumulation an interesting rule of thumb: ceteris paribus, two reasons pulling at the same direction are jointly stronger than each one of them alone.

Therefore, in the case of merely indirect (or "soft") reasons for the conclusion, they should accumulate, since several reasons considered together may outweigh another reason, as long as the former reasons are independent reasons and are not taken separately. This behaviour in weighing is known as the *accrual of reasons* Hage [1997]. An example of the accrual of reasons is found in Verheij [1994], and reproduced in Verheij [1995]:

■ EXAMPLE 1.4

Assume that John has robbed someone, so that he should be punished (α_1). Nevertheless, a judge decides that he should not be punished, because he is a first offender (β). Or, assume that John has injured someone, and should therefore be punished (α_2). Again, the judge decides he should not be punished, being a first offender (β). Now assume John has robbed and injured someone at the same time, so that there are two arguments for punishing him (α_1, α_2). In this case, the judge might decide that John should be punished, even though he is a first offender (β).

Notice that some authors speak of accrual of *reasons* Pollock [1991a] while others consider the cumulative pooling of information as accrual of *arguments* instead Verheij [1995]. I rather prefer to treat both concepts as they are of different kinds. In legal argumentation, *reasons* may be accumulated, so too the *arguments* as well. Reasons are unconditioned propositions without the *if-then* clause, while arguments are conditioned propositions. An example of the former we find in factual evidence, moral principles and values; An example of the latter occurs when one combines several arguments for an outcome.

In this dissertation, I am primarily concerned with the first kind of accrual, hoping that the formalism will be expressive enough to also capture the accrual of arguments. But this feature remains to be investigated, jointly with an argumentation framework for the system proposed in this dissertation.

Some authors (cf. Pollock [1995] have argued that combining reasons is not a matter of inference but rather it is a problem of formulating premises. As far as I see, this phenomenon is actually related to the inference relation. If we consider the accrual of reasons as a matter of formulating premises, one could argue that reasoning with incomplete information (nonmonotonic reasoning) can also be seen as a problem of formulating premises. Haskell Curry (see Curry [1977]), admitting the revision of the set of premises to distinguish philosophical logic from mathematical logic, shows his concerns about formulating premises, to avoid the "error" which leads to a revision of the conclusions:

> We observe that we reason, in the sense that we draw conclusions from our data; that sometimes these conclusions are correct, sometimes not; and that sometimes these errors are explained by the fact that some of our data were mistaken, but not always; and gradually we become aware that reasonings conducted according to certain norms can be depended on if the data are correct.

However, the revisability of premises (that is, the "error" of the data) is the main feature of nonmonotonic reasoning, and if we regard this problem as a matter of formulating premises, we do not need a nonmonotonic logic at all. In the same way, the *accrual of reasons* is not a matter of formulating premises, as long as we do have premises with independent reasons that, together, should behave differently. Hence, the accrual of reason is clearly an inference problem, and a logical system must be flexible enough to deal with different independent reasons for a conclusion, such it does with dependent reasons.

An open question in the literature is whether the weighing and balancing can be fully formalized in logic. Some authors Peczenik [1989] Sieckmann [2003] claim that it is not possible yet, despite the state-of-the-art of the research in logic, while others claim that it is already possible, proposing a weight formula Alexy [2003]. Nevertheless, a logical structure for modelling weighing and balancing (practical reasoning) is a very significant issue.

In recent years, several systems of deviant logics and also extensions of classical logic have been introduced. In particular, systems of nonmonotonic logics and defeasible reasoning were developed to deal with incomplete and inconsistent information, both in computer science (Goldszmidt and Pearl [1991a], Geffner [1992], Lehmann [1995] etc.) and in legal reasoning (Prakken [1997], Hage [1997], Verheij [1996], Sartor [1994] etc.). I shall claim in section 3.3.3 that weighing and balancing can be modelled in a conditional logic, notably in Lehmann's Lexicographic Closure (a logic described in nonmonotonic literature), as long as we extend this logic (as I shall describe), and if the reasons for and the reasons against a state of affairs are known and have been used in the argumentation framework. Therefore, the reconstruction of the weighing structure will be logically possible.

CHAPTER 2

NONMONOTONIC REASONING

"Γνωμαι πλεον κρατουσιν η σϑενοςχερων."
(*Plain reasonings tie hardy than powerful hands*).

—Sofocles, *939 Radt*

2.1 A Conceptual Sketch on Nonmonotonic Reasoning

In mathematics, a consequence derived by deduction from a set of premisses still is derived by the same deduction from a expanded set of premisses. The deduction remains valid, and it does not matter whether a new premiss was added to the knowledge base. This reasoning is called *monotonic* and keeps the mathematical proof as definitive and independent of new information. Thus, theorems with complete proofs are never invalid on the basis of later knowledge. A calculus of deductive systems with such features was introduced by Tarski, and the monotone functions can be found in the well-known *Knaster-Tarski theorem* Tarski [1955], capturing the general concept of a monotonic formal system.

In Gentzen notation, we can represent monotonic consequence as:

$$\text{If } \Gamma \vdash \tau, \text{ then } \Gamma, \sigma \vdash \tau$$

Let us take the following example to illustrate a *monotonic* deduction, with the operation known as *detachment* (the *modus ponens* scheme of inference). From the axioms *Socrates is a man* and *All men are mortal* we derive the theorem *Socrates is mortal*. In First Order Predicate Calculus we have:

$$\frac{\forall x.Man(x) \supset Mortal(x), Man(S)}{Mortal(S)}$$

In monotonic reasoning the theorem $Mortal(S)$ will always be deducible, even when we enlarge the set of premises with a new axiom. For instance, if we add the axiom *Socrates is Greek* the previously derived theorem still holds. Formally,

$$\frac{\forall x.Man(x) \supset Mortal(x), Man(S), Greek(S)}{Mortal(S)}$$

However, there exists another form of reasoning suggested by Minsky (see Minsky [1975]) which is more adequate to legal domain. This reasoning sanctions a deduction of a sentence in the absence of evidence against it. The derived sentence belongs to the category of *beliefs* instead of *truth*. Thus, adding a new premiss to the set of beliefs can invalidate a previously derived conclusion. This reasoning is called *nonmonotonic*.

Non-monotonic reasoning thus is a form of dealing with uncertainty usually found in common sense, and it consists in drawing conclusions from a set of *rules* which may have exceptions, and from a set of *facts* which is often incomplete. The belief set formed by both rules and facts is assumed by default and can be revised whenever new evidence is added. In such a case, the sentences previously entailed should be withdraw even though the rules continue belonging to our set of beliefs. Technically, we describe it as follows:

$$\text{If } \Gamma \vdash \tau, \text{ then } \Gamma, \sigma \not\vdash \tau.$$

Let us consider, for instance, the most quoted example in nonmonotonic reasoning. From the premises *"Tweety is a bird"* and *"All birds fly"* we derive the theorem *"Tweety flies"*. However, this theorem should no longer be derived if we consider the information that *"Tweety is a penguin"*, because albeit *"penguins are birds"*, we know that *"penguins do not fly"*. As long as Tweety is an exceptional bird (a penguin), it cannot fly. Classical logics do not deal with belief revision, and the previous conclusion will always be sanctioned. In a word, classical logics are monotonic. Nonmonotonic logics, otherwise, were developed to capture the reasoning under incomplete or inconsistent information.

Legal reasoning is a domain where nonmonotonicity is a highly desirable property. Legal norms are subject to exceptions and the information that justifies the application of a legal norm is characterized by uncertainty or by incompleteness. Furthermore, in legal domain one can hardly find a norm which has no exception at all. Let us take the following intuitive example regarding Criminal Law[1]. From the premises *"Homicide yields criminal liability"* and *"John Doe killed somebody"*, we derive *"John Doe has criminal liability"*. However, this consequence should no longer be derived if one adds to the knowledge base the premiss *"John Doe killed in self-defense"*, because *"self-defense does not yield criminal liability"*. On the other hand, even the last consequence should no longer be derived if another premiss is added, as when the death was caused with "malice aforethought", that is, when the actor had intent to kill. So, nonmonotonic reasoning is an essential property of legal domain, although this kind of reasoning procedure in law has always stayed on a rather insecure informal level, until recently (Prakken [1997], Hage [1997], Verheij [1996], Gordon [1993a], etc.).

Therefore, the deducibility of legal consequences usually demands a *jump* over unknown premises (cf. Peczenik [1989], discussed on Section 1.3.2 of Chapter 1), as a consequence of the open texture of legal concepts. The open texture is related to uncertainty, and to the incompleteness of the set of facts. Since these properties are found in common sense reasoning, in which nonmonotonic techniques aim to capture, it was natural to investigate nonmonotonic techniques to provide a calculus of legal reasoning, in a way to settle the entailed consequences albeit the uncertainty over the premises. Therefore, it is reassuring to know that the attempt to formalize the reasoning procedure in law with nonmonotonic logics was just a matter of time. Indeed, some nonmonotonic logics was even developed to deal with legal reasoning (see Prakken and Sartor [1996], Gordon [1993b], Hage [1997], Lodder [1999], Branting [2000] to name but a few).

In the next Subsection we briefly discuss about uncertainty, a property that characterizes common sense reasoning and, likewise, legal reasoning.

2.1.1   On Certainty and Belief

A characteristic of the human reasoning is that roughly speaking, knowledge can be represented to refer to some objects and relations, in conjunction with the representation of the knowledge about their properties. The reasoning procedure is characterized by the inference over the objects and relations represented in a knowledge base. In classical logic, however, it is not possible to consider the whole set of objects and relations that are accounted for as such. A criticism to a logical representation of certainty is that logic needs a complete definition such that

$$\forall x.P(x) \supset x = a_1 \lor x = a_2 \lor x = a_3$$

Intuitively, it means that a behavior is a crime if and only if it is a murder or a physical harm or a robbery. All else will not be considered as crime. This approach fails because the assumed completeness is not really complete, since there are other behaviors that are also crimes. And even if we assume this definition as complete, it

---

[1] Some necessary premises were omitted.

will be imperfect. Not all physical harm can be classified as a crime, e.g., a medical physical harm to heal the patient, a self-defense situation, etc.

Hence, such complete definition fails for mainly three reasons Russell and Norvig [1995]: (i) it is often not possible to list the complete set of antecedent or consequents; (ii) *Theoretical Ignorance*, since frequently there is not a complete theory for the domain; (iii) *Practical Ignorance* in account we may not know a particular information, even when all the rules are known. In Legal Theory, one should regard Theoretical Ignorance as related with uncertainty of legal norms, and Practical Ignorance with incompleteness of the set of facts.

2.1.1.1 *Uncertainty and Rationality of Decisions*   Uncertainty have a direct influence upon a decision theory, and also upon what can be seen as a *'rational decision'*. For instance, take a legal norm prescribing an obligatory behavior that human beings ought to behave so and a sanction to the opposite behavior. A rational decision must seek a way to guarantee the fulfillment of the obligation, avoiding the threatened coercive act, that is, there is a preference for the state space which fulfills the obligation and avoid the sanction. In teleological reasoning, we can say that a rational decision looks for a *plan* that satisfies the *goal* of the norm.

Under uncertainty, however, is not possible to know which actions will prevent the sanction of a not fulfilled obligation, or which plans generates the successful goal of a teleological reasoning. Therefore, uncertainty makes it more hard to know which decisions can be considered rational.

For instance, assume that one has a contractual obligation to transport some goods from one location to another, delivering them by the end of every month. Presuppose now that, with a set of actions A_1 one has a 95 % chance of fulfill the contract by deadline. The question is: choosing the set of actions A_1 is a rational decision? What if there are other sets of actions $A_2, ..., A_n$, with higher probabilities of success, and even with lower costs? Consider, for example, that A_1 implies in reaching the destination with two months in advance. In this case, it will involve an undesirable storage cost, and A_1 is no longer a rational decision. A_2 may involve a route longer but faster than A_1, and so forth.

Hence, there exist *preferences* between the several plans or set of actions that achieves a goal, or even a deontic modality, according to the consequences of such actions. The preferences are evaluations between the different possible outcomes of the plans, i.e., between epistemic states that include all circumstances such as the fulfilment of obligations, the achievement of goals, the time of arriving, the costs of involved actions and so forth.

Remark that in situations where all the circumstances necessary to the fulfillment of an obligation or to the achievement of the goal are known, we may have a hard solving problem. However, when the complete set of acts are not known at all, the problem becomes still worse.

To reason with preferences, the literature (viz. Russell and Norvig [1995] talks about an utility theory, where utility means *'the quality of being useful'*. Utility theories thus involve an evaluation of states according to the degree of usefulness (utility) of each state. A state S_i with higher utility is preferred to a state S_{n+1} with lower utility.

Two features of utility theory worth a note. First, the utility of a state is relative to the subject capable of epistemic states, whose preferences are represented by the utility function. The preference for a state where the tax is paid is obviously different for the taxpayer and for the National Treasury. A Murderer could have preference for a plea bargain with a light punishment while an innocent could prefer the trial, expecting to be set free of criminal charge. Therefore, a preference itself cannot be understood as rationality *senso stricto*, since there is no accounting for preferences. A subject capable of epistemic states who prefers not to pay tax should be considered misguided, but not irrational; a preference for suffering a penalty instead of fulfilling a contract cannot be thought of as irrational, as long as a preference for a type of car instead of another type cannot be irrational. An irrational decision is thus a decision for a state with lower expected utility, that is, states with lower degrees of usefulness. Second, utility theory allows for *'altruism'*, i.e., assigning high utility to states where others profit over the agent's own utility.

The axioms of utility[2] say nothing about utility itself. They talk about preferences instead.

Definition 13 *A utility function U maps states to real numbers such that*

$$U(A) > U(B) \quad \textit{iff A is preferred to B}$$
$$U(A) = U(B) \quad \textit{iff the agent is indifferent between A and B}$$

Definition 14 *The Maximum Expected Utility is the sum of the probabilities of each outcome times the utility of that outcome:*

$$U([p_1, S_1; ...; p_n, S_n]) = \sum_i p_i U(S_i)$$

A decision theory is formulated by combining probability theory and utility theory. In other words, evaluating an action by weighing the utility of a particular state by the probability that it occurs.

Definition 15 *A decision ψ is rational if and only if it chooses the action that yields the highest expected utility, averaged over all the possible states.*

Nevertheless, a decision ψ is not so easy to be generated. It may have a high computational cost if there are a large set of epistemic states and preference relations. However, in despite of the high cost, the true problem arises when we do not know by certainty about the set of the states that decision theory should be based on. In a word: the problem arises on account of the uncertainty of the set of epistemic states. Thus, a decision theory must be flexible enough to deal with uncertainty.

---

[2]The axioms of utility are Orderability, Transitivity, Continuity, Substitutability, Monotonicity and Decomposability.

Qualitative decision theories, as opposed to quantitative theories, substitute quantitative measures that characterize probability theory by a qualitative measure. I shall return to this issue in section 2.2.2.

2.1.1.2 Uncertainty and Nonmonotonic Reasoning

Generally, it is customary to say that common sense reasoning involves *'jumping to conclusions'*. Consider the most quoted example in nonmonotonic literature. We should expect to conclude that Tweety can fly, as long as we know that Tweety is a bird, according to the general rule that birds can fly. For this conclusion however, the full set of circumstances was not considered, and the decision can be revised if we know later that Tweety is an exceptional bird that does not fly, e.g., an ostrich or a penguin.

So, nonmonotonic reasoning allows for *'jumping to conclusions'* in the absence of the complete set of information about the domain, that is, it allows reasoning under uncertainty. It should be noted that the conclusion obtained through nonmonotonic logics is not possible in classical logic, that consider the consequence relation as definitive and monotone.

In nonmonotonic reasoning the conclusion can be revised in the presence of new evidence. Uncertainty is closely related with revisability and fallibility. According to Spohn [1994], certainty is at least a tuple of the form: the subject a is certain of proposition p at time t to the degree r. He claims that such relation asks for a subject capable of epistemic attitudes, a proposition or another object of belief, a time interval, and a degree of belief. The belief that a subject has about the proposition can continuously change.

Certainty therein is an epistemic state subject to a continuously revision, since our beliefs can change on account of new evidence or information. Such dynamics of epistemic change only is embedded if we assign a degree of belief or certainty to the propositions. So, when we revise our beliefs, what is changed is the assignments of degrees, and not the propositions themselves.

A working theoretical model is decision theory acquainted by Jeffrey [1965], as the version developed by Savage [1954]. For a comparision of decision theoretic models, see Spohn [1978]. The most prominent theoretical model is through representing epistemic states as probability measures, in mathematical sense, as in Jeffrey's generalized conditionalization Jeffrey [1965] and Hunter's maximizing entropy or minimizing relative entropy Hunter [1991].

Some alternatives to the probabilistic model are the so-called AGM postulates Alchourrón et al. [1985], the theory of ranking functions or ordinal conditional functions Spohn [1988], Goldszmidt and Pearl [1992], the Dempster-Shafer theory of belief functions Shafer [1976], Shafer [1990] and fuzzy logic Dubois and Prade [1988], among other works.

2.1.2 Nonmonotonic Systems

There are some systems which behavior are regarded as nonmonotonic. These systems provide an understanding of the properties of inferences in non-monotonic reasoning, allowing a comprehension of the desired behavior of non-monotonic logics.

So, I shall give a brief revision in such systems.

2.1.2.1 *Closed-World Assumption* Closed-World Assumption is a simple method where every information not present in a knowledge base is assumed to be false. For example, if a legal knowledge base does not have any information about a norm that obliges one to keep his(her) dog leashed than it is assumed that such an obligation does not exist. Hence, the negation of the information is added to the closure of the knowledge base. To be more specific, if a ground term cannot be inferred, then its negation is added to the closure of the knowledge base.

Definition 16 *A Knowledge Base KB is assumed closed, CWA(KB), if and only if*

$$CWA(KB) = KB \cup \{\neg P(t) | KB \not\models P(t)\}$$

where $P(t)$ is a ground predicate formula.

Since the rule *'one ought to keep his/her dog leashed'* is not a logical consequence of the knowledge base, the database must be augmented with the information that *'one not ought to keep his/her dog leashed'*, because all instances of a relation are assumed to be deducible from the knowledge base.

The non-monotonic behavior of the Closed-World Assumption occurs in the addition of new information to the knowledge base. In such a case, the knowledge base not only supports the new information but also replaces the old ones, that denies the occurrence not admitted before. Hence, the addition of a information *'one ought to keep his/her dog leashed'* replaces its negation on the knowledge base.

The problem with CWA is that the information could be inconsistent with reasonable KB Brewka *et al.* [1997]. For instance, assume a KB with a disjunctive formula $\sigma \lor \tau$. Since neither σ nor τ is deducible from the KB, both $\neg\sigma$ and $\neg\tau$ are added to the closure what is inconsistent with $\sigma \lor \tau$. A way to avoid such inconsistency is regarding the KB as *definite* Clark [1978], i.e., when a clause is converted to a conjunctive normal form (CNF), it contains at most one positive literal (Horn clauses). In predicate calculus the definitiveness of a predicate P is reached by "closing off " a theory. Thus, a theory $\forall x.A(x) \supset P(x)$ is *completed* with the axiom $\forall x.P(x) \supset A(x)$ becoming $\forall x.P(x) \equiv A(x)$.

Closed-World Assumption also assumes *Unique Name Assumption* and *Domain Closure Assumption*. By the former, different names are assumed to refer to different individuals, i.e., the terms are unique:

$$UNA : \{t_i \neq t_j | t_i \text{ and } t_j \text{ are distinct names}\}$$

By the latter, the number of individuals is assumed as finite and named:

$$DCA : \{t_i | \forall x.t_1 = x \lor t_2 = x \lor ... \lor t_n = x \text{ and } 1 \leq i \leq n\}$$

2.1.2.2 *Inheritance Network* Inheritance Networks are a restricted form of semantic networks and are concerned with a knowledge representation through directed graphs, by which each link represents relations among concepts, and which

animal

bird ⟶ fly

eagle   penguin

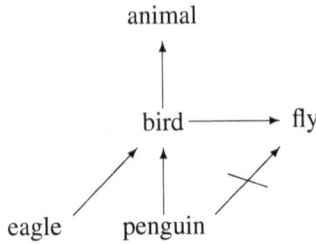

Figure 2.1   Example of Inheritance Network

the only admissible relation is that of class inclusion. Inheritance Networks have two types of links: (i) positive links ($\rightarrow$), denoting that one class is a subclass of another (e.g., birds fly); and (ii) negative links ($\nrightarrow$), denoting that one class is not a subclass of the complement of another (e.g., penguins do not fly). In the Inheritance Network depicted in figure 2.1, *eagle* inherits the properties of the superclass *bird*, i.e., *eagle flies* and is an *animal*. Penguin also inherits the properties of the superclass *bird*, however, it does not inherit the property *fly*, because there is a negative link to this property. Classes *inherit* the properties of their super-classes unless there exists a specified negative link to that property.

The nonmonotonicity property of Inheritance Network comes from its ability of retraction of conclusions, in the presence of new information. An important feature of Inheritance Network is the preference of *specific* subclasses over more *general* ones, revealing the specificity relation that drives most nonmonotonic formalisms.

2.1.2.3 *Logic Programming*

Another system that produces a nonmonotonic behaviour is Logic Programming. The syntax of Logic Programming has a nonempty set A of *atoms*, also called *positive literals*. A *negative literal* is an atom preceded by the classical negation symbol $\neg$, which forms the complement of the *positive literal*. For instance, $\neg A$ is the *complement* of A. A set of literals is said to be *inconsistent* if it contains both a literal and its complement, and *consistent* otherwise. A *basic rule* is an ordered pair *Head* $\leftarrow$ *Body*, whose *Head* is a literal, and whose *Body* is a finite set of literals. A basic rule with the Head L_0 and Body L_i, $1 \leq i \leq k$, can be represented as

$$L_0 \leftarrow L_1, L_2, ..., L_k$$

A Basic program is a set of basic rules. For instance, if A is $\{p, q, r, s\}$ then the rules

$$p,$$
$$\neg q,$$
$$r \leftarrow p,q,$$
$$\neg r \leftarrow p, \neg q, \tag{2.1}$$
$$s \leftarrow r,$$
$$s \leftarrow p,s,$$
$$\neg s \leftarrow p, \neg q, \neg r$$

form a basic program. Since every atom is used in the program at least once, it is not necessary to specify the set of atoms A explicitly, as long as it is presumed that all atoms used in the rules are in the set A.

The Consequence Relation in Logic Programming differs from classical logic. In classical logic, the *consequences* of a set of sentences Γ are the sentences that can be derived from Γ and from some *logical axioms* using some *inference rules*. In other words, the *consequences* of Γ is the smallest set of sentences that contains Γ and the logical axioms and is closed under the inference rules. Nevertheless, in logic programming, the *consequences* are literals that follow from a set of literals only when they *belong* to this set[3], that is, if Γ is consistent and a literal L is a consequence of Γ then $L \in \Gamma$.

Definition 17 *Let Γ be a set of literals. Γ is* logically closed *if it is consistent or equals to the set of literals. Γ is* closed *under a basic program Π iff, for every rule $Head \leftarrow Body$ in Π, $Head \in \Gamma$ whenever $Body \subseteq \Gamma$. The* consequence relation $Cn(\Pi)$ *is denoted by the smallest set of literals which is both logically closed and closed under Π, that is, the least fixpoint of a certain monotone function.*

For instance, the basic program of Equation 2.1 generates as consequences the set $\{p, \neg q, \neg r, \neg s\}$, which is logically closed and closed under Equation 2.1. It should be noted that replacing the rule $\neg s \leftarrow p, \neg q, \neg r$ in (2.1) by its "contrapositive" $r \leftarrow p, \neg q, s$ would change the consequences of the program, and the literal $\neg s$ would not be among the consequences anymore. So, the contrapositive does not hold in logic programming, as it occurs on conditionals in classical logic.

Negation as failure is a form of negation where negative literals are assumed to be derivable when every derivation for the atom fails (cf. Clark [1978]). This form of negation produces a nonmonotonic behaviour because a derivation success when new information becomes available and fails in its absence. For instance, if the program Π has a single rule $p \leftarrow$ not q, the negation as failure yields p. But when the rule $q \leftarrow$ is added to Π, p can be derived no longer.

This leads to the definition of *rule element* which is a literal possibly preceded by the negation as failure symbol *not*. For any set Γ of literals, the set $\{$not $\Delta : \Delta \in \Gamma\}$ is denoted by $not(\Gamma)$. Then the rules can be represented as $Head \leftarrow Pos \cup not(Neg)$, for some finite sets of literals Pos, Neg, or

---

[3]Except on the trivial case when the set is inconsistent.

$$L_0 \leftarrow L_1, ..., L_m, not\ L_{m+1}, ..., not\ L_n.$$

The symbol *not* "blocks" the application of the rules that contains negation as failure literals in its body, whenever the literal assumed not in the set of literals is added to the program.

A feature of negation as failure is that, in some semantics, it makes a program "nondeterministic", that is, there can be several "correct" ways to organize the process of deriving literals using rules that contains negation as failure. Each of them produces a different set of literals.

2.1.2.4 Truth Maintenance Systems

Doyle's Truth Maintenance Systems (Doyle [1979]) keeps track of dependencies among propositions. The user expresses justifications among propositions, and the system generates a labeling IN or OUT, meaning that the proposition is believed (has a valid justification) or not (has not a valid justification), respectively. Each justification is made in an IN-list and an OUT-list. Validity is reached when each proposition in the IN-list and no proposition in OUT-list has a valid justification. Circularities are blocked by requiring that the admissible labelings are to be *well-founded*, that is, to be *minimal* in the set of propositions.

The syntax of Truth Maintenance Systems is

$$\text{IN-list} \mid \text{OUT-list} \rightarrow \text{atom} \qquad (2.2)$$

An example of a Truth Maintenance System are the following justifications:

$$
\begin{aligned}
&J_1 : T \mid M \rightarrow P \\
&J_2 : L \mid \rightarrow M \\
&J_3 : \quad \rightarrow T
\end{aligned}
\qquad (2.3)
$$

The justification J_1 says that if John Doe is a thief (T) and is not believed that he is a minor (M), then he ought to be punished (P); J_2 says that if John Doe is less than 18 years old (L), then he is a minor; J_3 says that John Doe is a thief.

Within these justifications, the TMS will label the atoms T and P as IN and M as OUT. However, if a new justification $J_4 : \quad \rightarrow L$ ("John Doe is less than 18 years old") is added, then M will become IN, defeating the justification for P and forcing P to be labeled as OUT. Therefore, P ("John Doe ought to be punished") does not hold anymore.

The literature (cf. Geffner [1992]) has shown that Doyle's TMS is not very different from propositional logic programming, and that the admissible TMS labelings correspond to the stable models of logic programming.

Thus, each TMS justification of the form $p_1, ..., p_n \mid q_1, ..., q_m \rightarrow p$ can be mapped into a rule of the form $p \leftarrow p_1, ..., p_n, not\ q_1, ..., not\ q_m$.

2.1.2.5 Time Map Management Systems

Time Map Management Systems were described in Dean and McDermott [1987] and Hanks and McDermott [1985]. These systems reason about propositions which change over time. In an informal description, TMMS infers that a proposition holds at a later time, after a sequence of events has occurred. If there is no change in the set of beliefs, the propositions are assumed to persist. The changes are considered as a result of events whose effects are described through causal rules. For instance, a rule may say that John Doe ought to pay taxes if he had profit; another rule may indicate that if John Doe has not paid taxes at a certain period of time t, he will get a fine at time $t + \Delta$.

Starting from the point of time it has complete information, the system moves on looking for causal rules that holds, updating the database accordingly.

Time Map Management Systems may have a very interesting behavior on reasoning about temporal deontic logic, which is interesting for legal reasoning. However, we are first concerned about a *logic* for nonmonotonic reasoning, and we are not going to analyze such systems.

2.1.3 Non-monotonic Logics

Curiously, the three seminal formalisms for non-monotonic reasoning were introduced at almost the same time. The Journal *Artificial Intelligence*, Volume 13, ns. 1-2 (1980), contains the articles where Circumscription, Default Logic, and (Modal) Non-Monotonic Logic were first described. I shall give an insight on the three formalisms, as an attempt of accomplish the understanding on these logics.

2.1.3.1 *Circumscription*   According to McCarthy (cf. McCarthy [1980]), *circumscription* is defined as:

> a rule of conjecture that can be used by a person or a program for "jumping to certain conclusions". Namely, the objects that can be shown to have a certain property P by reasoning from certain facts A are all the objects that satisfy P.

Circumscription incorporates fundamental concepts as *negation as failure*, developed in logic programming Clark [1978] and *close world assumption* from database theory Reiter [1978]. It is obtained by means of extending a first order theory by minimizing the extensions of certain predicates. Thus, the objects that satisfy a predicate P are exactly the objects which can be *shown* to satisfy P. Working with an example, take a database with only the fact $Q(a)$; the circumscription of Q thus will permit us to generate the formula $\forall x.Q(x) \Rightarrow x = a$, that is, a is the only object that satisfies Q. Therefore, if b is different from a, circumscription will allow us to "jump to the conclusion" $\neg Q(b)$. However, if $Q(b)$ is learned, a new conclusion will be obtained, that is, would be those derivable from the formula $\forall x.Q(x) \Leftrightarrow x = a \vee x = b$. In this point, circumscription behaviors like close-world-assumption. Formally, circumscription can be expressed in the following terms:

Definition 18 *McCarthy [1980] Given a first order sentence $A(P)$ containing the predicate P, and a sentence $A(\Phi)$ resulting from the replacement of all predicate P by the predicate Φ with the same arity of P, them the circumscription $Circ[A(P); P]$ of P in $A(P)$ is expressed as the second order schema*

$$A(P) \wedge A(\Phi) \wedge \forall x.[\Phi(x) \Rightarrow P(x)] \Rightarrow \forall x.(P(x) \Rightarrow \Phi(x)) \qquad (2.4)$$

■ **EXAMPLE 2.1**

Consider the sentence $A(Q) : Q(a)$ and assume that the predicate $\Phi(x)$ is substituted by $x = a$. The circumscriptive schema generates the following closed first order formula:

$$Q(a) \wedge a = a \wedge \forall x.[x = a \Rightarrow Q(x)] \Rightarrow \forall x.Q(x) \Rightarrow x = a \qquad (2.5)$$

from which it yields a minimal definition of Q:

$$\forall x.Q(x) \Leftrightarrow x = a \qquad (2.6)$$

Recall that, in classical logic, a proposition φ is entailed by a sentence $A(P)$ if and only if φ holds in every model of $A(P)$. Circumscription has a weak notion of entailment, that is, a proposition φ is entailed by $Circ[A(P); P]$ if and only if φ holds in every model of $A(P)$ which is *minimal* in P. A model M is said to be minimal when the model preserves the same domain and interpretation of symbols, and if there is no other model with a smaller extension of P.

The nonmonotonic feature of circumscription arises from the constraints imposed by a set of axioms that produces a minimal interpretation for some predicate P. Circumscription will select a different minimal interpretation if the base of axioms changes. For instance, in example (2.1), $\neg Q(b)$ can be inferred. Nevertheless, if $Q(b)$ is added to the base of axioms, the circumscriptive schema selects $\forall x.Q(x) \Leftrightarrow x = a \vee x = b$, and $\neg Q(b)$ does not hold anymore.

Defeasible knowledge is encoded in circumscription as formulas $\forall x.bird(x) \wedge \neg ab_i(x) \Rightarrow flies(x)$, that is, "every *non-abnormal* bird flies" McCarthy [1986]. Hence, the inferential import of circumscription follows, according to McCarthy, from "minimizing abnormality", i.e., from circumscribing the predicates ab_i.

Circumscription is widely accepted due to its mathematical structure and on account of being based on first order logic. There have been many variations such that prioritised circumscription McCarthy [1986] and pointwise circumscription Lifschitz [1986]. Circumscription has been also used in conjunction with the situation calculus McCarthy [1986], the event calculus Kowalski and Sergot [1986] and temporal logics Shoham [1988]. For a survey on circumscription, see Lifschitz [1994].

2.1.3.2 Default Logic   Default logic was introduced by Reiter [1980], and treats defaults (defeasible knowledge) as inference rules with an additionl consistency check. Default theory is defined as a pair $\langle D, W \rangle$, where W is a set of first order formulas representing the facts which are known for certainty, and D is a set of defaults of the form

$$\frac{\alpha(x) : \beta_1(x), ..., \beta_n(x)}{\gamma(x)}$$

or in an alternative notation

$$\alpha(x) : \beta_1(x), ..., \beta_n(x)/\gamma(x)$$

that means: if α is provable and, for all i, $1 \leq i \leq n$, $\neg\beta_i$ is not provable, then derive γ. α is the precondition, β_i the test condition or justification, and γ the consequent. For instance, consider the following default theory:

$$D : \begin{cases} bird(x) : canfly(x)/canfly(x), \\ penguin(x) : \neg canfly(x)/\neg canfly(x) \end{cases}$$

$$W : \{bird(Tweety)\}$$

As long as $canfly(Tweety)$ is consistent with the Default Theory $T = \langle D, W \rangle$, we can derive $canfly(Tweety)$. However, if we add $penguin(Tweety)$ to the set of facts W, then the consistency check for applying the first default fails, and $canfly(Tweety)$ is no longer supported.

To deal with blocked defaults, Reiter introduced the notion of *extensions* of a Default Theory $T = \langle D, W \rangle$. An extension E must satisfy some features:

1. the facts in W must be contained in E, $W \subseteq E$, since they are known by certainty,

2. the extension E must be deductively closed in the sense of classical logic, $Th(E) = E$, because a reasoner does not only believe of the facts in W, but also in everything which logically follows from the defaults applied,

3. all defaults applicable to E must have been applied,

4. every formula in E must be derivable from W and the consequents of applied defaults in a non-circular way.

Here it was used the Tarski inclusion relation $Th(X) = X$ denoting the consequences of X instead of Gentzen inference relation $X \vdash X$. The main difference of both Notations rests on the set of consequences: while in Tarski-style involves the infinite set of consequences, the Gentzen-style is limited to finite sets.

Thus, an extension is a maximal set of well-formed formulas which includes W and every consequent γ of defaults $\alpha : \beta/\gamma$ in D for which $\alpha \in E$ and $\beta \notin E$.

Definition 19 *Reiter [1980] Given a closed default theory $T = \langle W, D \rangle$ and a set E of closed wff's, an extension is a sequence of sets $E_0, ..., E_i$ such that*

$$E_0 = W$$

and for $i \geq 0$

$$E_{i+1} = Th(E_i \cup \{\gamma | \alpha : \beta/\gamma \in D, \alpha \in E_i \text{ and } \neg\beta \notin E\})$$

then E is an extension of $T = \langle W, D \rangle$ iff

$$E = \bigcup_{i=0}^{\infty} E_i$$

Thus, the extension E_0 receives all formulas that are in the set of facts W and in each interation, it adds the consequence γ of the default $\alpha : \beta/\gamma$, iff the antecedent α is in the extension and the negation of the justification β is not an element of the extension E. So, an extension E of a default theory is the minimal fixed-point or a reiterated application of the theory to each default that belongs to D.

A default theory can generate inconsistent extensions. Let us see a legal example to formalize a nonmonotonic behavior with these semantics.

■ **EXAMPLE 2.2**

Let $T = \langle W, D \rangle$ be a default theory, where

$$D : \begin{cases} d_1 = Kill(x) : Penalty(x)/Penalty(x), \\ d_2 = SelfDefence(x) : \neg Penalty(x)/\neg Penalty(x) \end{cases}$$

$$W : \{SelfDefence(John), \forall x.SelfDefence(x) \supset Kill(x)\}$$

Both defaults cannot be simultaneously applied, since their consequences are inconsistent. Thus, if the default d_1 is applied, its consequence $Penalty$ will be added to the extension, and this will block up the default d_2. On the other hand, if we apply in the first place the default d_2, the consequence $\neg Penalty$ will be added to the extension, blocking up the default d_1. Consequently, this theory yields two extensions:

$$E_1 = Th(W \cup \{Penalty\})$$
$$E_2 = Th(W \cup \{\neg Penalty\})$$

The existence of multiple extensions results in two consequence notions. If a formula is in some extensions of a default theory, we have credulous reasoning, and alternatively if it is in all extensions then we say it as skeptical reasoning. Formally,

Definition 20 *[Credulous and Skeptical Consequences] Given a default theory $T = \langle W, D \rangle$,*

$$T \mid\!\sim_s \varphi \qquad \text{iff } \varphi \text{ is in all extensions of } T$$
$$T \mid\!\sim_c \varphi \qquad \text{iff } \varphi \text{ is in some extensions of } T$$

where $\mid\!\sim_s$ stands for skeptical consequence relation and $\mid\!\sim_c$ for a credulous consequence relation.

To deal with multiple extensions, Reiter and Criscuolo [1981] use semi-normal defaults, although Reiter [1980] originally claimed that only normal defaults are needed. A default is normal iff the justification is identical to the conclusion, that is,

$$\alpha(x) : \beta(x)/\beta(x)$$

A default is semi-normal iff the justification contains the conclusion and also another formula, i.e.,

$$\alpha(x) : \beta(x) \wedge \gamma(x)/\beta(x)$$

Finally, a default is non-normal iff the justification is different from the conclusion:

$$\alpha(x) : \gamma(x)/\beta(x)$$

For instance, in example (2.2), we can use normal and semi-normal defaults, in the following:

$$T = \langle W, D' \rangle, \text{ where}$$

$$D' = \begin{cases} d'_1 = Kill(x) : \neg SelfDefence(x) \wedge Penalty(x)/Penalty(x) \\ d_2 = SelfDefence(x) : \neg Penalty(x)/\neg Penalty(x) \end{cases}$$

$$W = \{SelfDefence(John), \forall x.SelfDefence(x) \supset Kill(x)\}$$

This default theory yields now just one extension:

$$E = W \cup \{\neg Penalty\}$$

The representation of defaults as (nonstandard) inference rules gives to Reiter's Default Logic its powerful expressiveness. Nevertheless, the literature Brewka *et al.* [1997] has shown some problems that Default Logic does not solve, such that

1. EXISTENCE OF EXTENSIONS

   There is no guarantee that Default Logic yields extensions. Let us see an example. In default theory $\{true : \neg\varphi/\varphi\}$, if E does not contain the formula φ, then E is not an extension, since the default was not applied. On the other side, if E contains φ, then it will generate a set without φ because the default is not applicable with respect to E. Thus, E is not an extension.

2. REASONING BY CASES [Consequence notion too weak]

   It has been argued that Default Logic cannot reason by cases, as it is shown in the following example:

   $$D = \begin{cases} d_1 = Murderer(x) : Penalty(x)/Penalty(x) \\ d_2 = Thief(x) : Penalty(x)/Penalty(x) \end{cases}$$

   $$W = \{Murderer(John) \vee Thief(John)\}$$

   The only extension skeptically generated is

   $$Th(Murderer(John) \vee Thief(John))$$

   though we should expect that $Penalty(John)$ must be on the extension. One of the defaults should be applied whether the person is a murderer or a thief.

Thus, Default Logic inference relation violates Or, since the conclusion is not contained in all extensions.

The interested reader should see the analysis of Brewka *et al.* [1997], in terms of the metatheoretic properties of nonmonotonic inference relations, to avoid this problem.

3. JOINT CONSISTENCY OF EXTENSIONS [Consequence notion too strong]

Consider the following example, inspired on Poole [1989]:

$$D = \{true : Usable(x) \wedge \neg Broken(x)/Usable(x)\}$$
$$W = \{Broken(LeftArm) \vee Broken(RightArm)\}$$

The only extension contains

$$E = \{Usable(LeftArm) \wedge Usable(RightArm)\}$$

although one of the arms is broken.

This occurs because an extension only requires that each justification of an applied default is consistent with the generated extension, but does not demand a cumulative consistency of all justifications of all applied defaults.

4. CUMULATIVITY

The consequence relation $\vdash\!\!\sim$ of Default Logic does not satisfy Cumulativity, as was demonstrated by Makinson [1989], in the following example:

$$(1)true : p/p$$
$$(2)p \vee q : \neg p/\neg p$$

The extension contains p what triggers the second default, since $p \vee q$ is its precondition. Thus, a second extension is generated containing $\neg p$, and therefore, is skeptically derivable no longer. We will return to cumulativity properties in Section 2.2.1

Several modifications and extensions in Default Logic were proposed in the literature Lukaszewicz [1988], Brewka [1991], Brewka [1994b], Brewka [1994a]. An interesting work was done by Etherington [1987], which proposes a model-theoretic semantics for Default Logic. The main idea of this approach is that all subsets of the set of models for W are ordered according to how well they satisfy the defaults, such that each maximal set in this ordering is the set of models for some extension. Notice that this theory gives a semantic interpretation of extensions, rather than of defaults.

2.1.3.3 Modal Non-Monotonic Logics Modal Non-Monotonic Logics is also based on a fixed-point equation, and it uses a modal operator to refer to their own consistency. The initial attempts to formulate these logics were from McDermott and Doyle (McDermott and Doyle [1980]).

McDermott and Doyle's Non-Monotonic Logic was based on the addition of a new operator M to the language of propositional logic, standing for consistency. Therefore, a sentence of the form *if someone kills somebody and it is consistent with not being in self-defence, he ought to be punished.* Formally,

$$(k \wedge M \neg sd \to p) \qquad (2.7)$$

However, the attempts in defining a semantic interpretation to the new constant M were unsatisfactory. A reconstruction of the modal operator as self-belief was then proposed by Moore's autoepistemic logic (Moore [1985]).

Autoepistemic Logic is an attempt to improve the seminal formalism using an epistemic interpretation. In this reinterpretation of the modal non-monotonic logic, propositional theories are augmented by a belief operator L, such that sentences of the form $L\varphi$ are read as φ *is believed*, or *it is known that φ*.

The intuition behind this interpretation is that a set of formulas is constructed on the basis of the premisses ('*base beliefes*' of the reasoner), containing *everything* the reasoner believes, either about the world or about its own beliefs. For instance, 2.7 is denoted in autoepistemic logic as follows:

$$(k \wedge \neg Lsd) \to p$$

Thus, in a propositional calculus one can derive that if there should be the penalty, since it is not known that the agent killed in self-defence, $\neg Lsd$. The nonmonotonic property holds since adding the sentence sd makes $\neg Lsd$ false. This behaviour is captured through the following conditions.

If an ideal introspective reasoner knows φ, then he/she also knows that he/she knows φ. On the other hand, if the reasoner does not know φ, then he/she at least knows that he/she does not know φ. Therefore, whether a set T contains all the reasoner knows, then φ belongs to T if and only if he/she knows φ, and φ does not belong to T if and only if he/she does not know φ. Formally

$$L\varphi \quad \text{iff } \varphi \in T$$
$$\neg L\varphi \quad \text{iff } \varphi \notin T$$

So, every set that contains these conditions, and is deductively closed, are called *stable sets*. A stable set is ground if and only if it captures the following fixed point property:

Definition 21 (Stable Expansion) *Given an autoepistemic theory T, a stable expansion is the sets of formulas $S(T)$ such that*

$$S(T) = Th(T + \{Lp : p \in S(T)\} + \{\neg Lp : p \notin S(T)\})$$

Finally, there has been a reconciliation of the autoepistemic logic with McDermott and Doyle's modal nonmonotonic logic, proposed by Marek and Truszczynski [1991].

2.1.4 Semantics: fixed-point or model-theoretic?

A much debated issue in the literature is whether non-monotonic logics should have a model-theoretic semantic or a proof-theoretic one, based on consistency checking.

Some logics were developed to nonmonotonic reasoning based on a consistency test, using the fixed point idea, such as Default Logic, Modal Nonmonotonic Logic, Autoepistemic Logic. Some authors also claimed that nonmonotonic reasoning needs no longer model theory, but a different kind of semantics instead. Such semantics should be based on checking the consistency among defaults in the set, adding to the theory as many conclusions of applicable defaults as possible.

Some researchers even argued that a more natural way to formalise nonmonotonic reasoning is through *argumentation-theoretic* semantics. Some authors such as Pollock [1991b], Vreeswijk [1993] and Loui [1998] advocate that the meaning of a defeasible sentence should not be seen as a correspondence with reality as in model theory, but instead in its role in dialectical inquiry.

The main idea of this approach is that the meaning of defeasible reasoning is not captured in terms of relating a proposition and the world and, thus, is not *propositional*. So, to capture the defeasibility of a relation between premises and conclusions of conditionals, it is necessary to induce a burden of proof. This is achieved by considering *attack* and *defeat* relations (viz. *rebuttal* and *undercutting*) among arguments (defeasible sentences). Therefore, the semantics of such *argumentation-theoretic* approach seek to capture as large as possible sets of arguments, that are adequately defended against attacks over their members. In other words, the semantics should generate a maximal set of defeasible sentences, using the consistency among their elements in defining the fixed-point.

This approach is called *proof-theoretic, fixed-point, consistency-based* logics [Brewka et al., 1997, pp. 3] or *argumentation theoretic* Prakken and Vreeswijk [2002].

On the other hand, model theory is traditionally used to define the meaning of a logical language by establishing its correspondence with the world. So, propositional formulas are regarded in correspondence with reality. Model-theoretic semantics thus tell the meaning of logical symbols (e.g., propositions in propositional calculus) by defining how the world apparently would be if these symbols would be true. Logical consequence (entailment) is defined as, given the premises are true, then the conclusion must show a representation of the world which is actually true.

In nonmonotonic reasoning, model theoretic semantics should tell us how the world normally, typically would be whenever a defeasible sentence is true. Entailment should be defined as the most normal worlds or models that satisfy the premises. It's easy to see that model-theoretic logics stay 'closer' to classical logic and have been keeping the attention os several reseachers.

It is not the purpose of this work to discuss whether fixed-point semantics are better than model-theoretic semantics or not, but instead to present the two approaches, since one of the semantics must be used to formalise legal reasoning. By the way, one may argue that in legal reasoning, legal debates could be more naturally captured through an *argumentation-theoretic* logic. It should be noted that among Artificial Intelligence and Law researchers, there is a preference for such an approach to capture legal reasoning, in attention to the recent Law Theories concerning argumentation (Alexy [1978], Perelman and Olbrechts-Tyteca [1969] among others). But this assertion does not deny the significance of *model-theoretic* semantics to capture legal reasoning. Some authors, like Prakken and Vreeswijk [2002], that advocate argumentation-theoretic logics, even point out that model-theoretic semantics should have a restricted usage, by defining the initial components of an argumentation system, the notions of a logical language and the consequence relation. Furthermore, an argumentation framework can be modeled also in model-theoretic semantics Gordon [1993b].

On the other hand, some authors (Geffner and Pearl [1992]) have introduced argumentation systems as proof theories for model-theoretic semantics of preferential entailment, making their system complete and sound.

Generally, the two approaches are often related. Excluding the case when a proof system is specially developed[4] to the semantics, one method remains as a proof of the other. Thus, according to [Brewka *et al.*, 1997, p. 5], usually model-preference logics (such as Closed-World Assumption, Circumscription, Conditional Logics) have consistency-based logics as proof methods (Negation-as-failure in Logic Programming, Argumentation System in Conditional Entailment), and conversely fixed-point logics (Default Logic, Modal Nonmonotonic Logics) have model-theoretic approaches as proof methods (Justification based Truth Maintenance Systems).

2.2 Model-theoretic semantics and Conditional Logics

2.2.1 Metatheoretic properties

Although several systems for performing nonmonotonic behaviour had been developed, a study of the theoretical properties of nonmonotonic reasoning was missing. This theoretical analysis was first suggested by Gabbay, which observed that, although not all of the classical logic's axioms hold for nonmonotonic logics, some subset of these axioms can be present in such logical system. Some important properties of provability operator[5] $\vdash$ are:

$$\text{Inclusion} \qquad \Gamma, \sigma \vdash \sigma$$

$$\text{Cut} \qquad \frac{\Gamma \vdash \tau \; \Gamma, \tau \vdash \sigma}{\Gamma \vdash \sigma}$$

---

[4]In Prakken [2000] a procedural proof method was built fot declarative fixed-point semantics. In such a proof method, a procedure is defined for testing whether an argument is a member of the set of arguments that is acceptable.

[5]Here the Gentzen inference operator is used instead of Tarski. In the Tarski notation, for instance, the inclusion relation $\Gamma \vdash \sigma$ is translated to $\sigma \in Th(\Gamma)$, where $Th(\Gamma)$ are the consequences of Γ.

$$\text{Monotony} \qquad \frac{\Gamma \vdash \sigma}{\Gamma, \tau \vdash \sigma}$$

In nonmonotonic reasoning, the *inclusion* axiom (reflexivity), which allows the deduction of the contents of its own knowledge base, is clearly expected:

$$\Gamma, \sigma \hspace{0.5mm}\mid\hspace{-1mm}\sim \sigma$$

Gabbay introduced the symbol $\mid\hspace{-1mm}\sim$ to replace $\vdash$ where the former denotes non-monotonic deducibility and the latter denotes classical provability.

Also looking for nonmonotonic theoretical properties, Makinson Makinson [1989] defined rules to *cumulative inferences*, that was referred to as *inclusion, cut (cumulative transitivity)* and *cautious monotony*:

Definition 22 (Cumulative Inference Relation) *An inference relation $\mid\hspace{-1mm}\sim$ is cumulative iff it satisfies:*

$$\text{Supraclassicality} \qquad \frac{\Gamma \vdash \sigma}{\Gamma \mid\hspace{-1mm}\sim \sigma}$$

$$\text{Inclusion} \qquad \Gamma, \sigma \mid\hspace{-1mm}\sim \sigma$$

$$\text{Cut} \qquad \frac{\Gamma \mid\hspace{-1mm}\sim \tau \quad \Gamma, \tau \mid\hspace{-1mm}\sim \sigma}{\Gamma \mid\hspace{-1mm}\sim \sigma}$$

$$\text{Cautious Monotony} \qquad \frac{\Gamma \mid\hspace{-1mm}\sim \tau, \; \Gamma \mid\hspace{-1mm}\sim \sigma}{\Gamma, \tau \mid\hspace{-1mm}\sim \sigma}$$

Then, the analysis was extended to include the propositional connective *or*, and the Cumulative systems that satisfy *or* are called *Preferential*:

Definition 23 (Preferential Inference Relation) *An inference relation $\mid\hspace{-1mm}\sim$ is preferential iff it is cumulative and satisfies:*

$$\frac{\Gamma, \sigma \mid\hspace{-1mm}\sim \phi \quad \Gamma, \tau \mid\hspace{-1mm}\sim \phi}{\Gamma, \sigma \vee \tau \mid\hspace{-1mm}\sim \phi}$$

Notice that both works are based on the proof theoretic properties of nonmonotonic reasoning. However, Shoham [1987] introduced a framework based on a model theoretic account. His *preferential logics* use a preference relation over the models of an underlying logic, be it propositional, first order or modal, such that particular preferred models are selected rather than having to consider all satisfying models.

Kraus, Lehmann and Magidor Kraus *et al.* [1990] extended this idea in a remarkable paper which is known as one of the seminal works on nonmonotonic reasoning, by proving the equivalence of a slight modification of Shoham's preferential logics and the provable properties of Makinson's cumulative inference. The result of this approach forms a sound and complete axiomatisation of nonmonotonic reasoning and has become known as P (standing for preferential or probabilistic[6]), also considered as the *core* of acceptable nonmonotonic behaviour (Geffner [1992]).

---

[6]It also stands for probabilistic since such rules are equivalent to those defined by Adams [1975].

System P sanctions only the consequences of preferential models thus keeping the specificity relations among defaults, nevertheless it fails in sanctioning irrelevant information from superclass to a subclass of defaults. Therefore, Lehmann and Magidor Lehmann and Magidor [1988], Lehmann and Magidor [1992] looked for a more complete system and added to P a further rule, called *rational monotonicity*:

Definition 24 (Rational Inference Relation) *An inference relation $\mid\!\sim$ is rational iff it is preferential and satisfies:*

$$\frac{\Gamma \mid\!\sim \phi \; \Gamma \mid\!\not\sim \neg\tau}{\Gamma, \tau \mid\!\sim \phi}$$

The rational behavior is obtained by restricting the preference relation in a total ordering over models (ranked preferential models), resulting in *rational consequence relations*. Then, a wide branch of nonmonotonic systems was developed based on the preferential and rational model semantics of Kraus *et al.* [1990] and Lehmann and Magidor [1992].

2.2.2 Ranking Functions and Kappa Calculus

Spohn (cf. Spohn [1988], Spohn [1990]) has argued that quantitative methods for handling uncertainty (that is, numerical probabilities), were inadequate to model epistemic beliefs and how they change when revised. The access to the underlying numerical values of quantitative methods is neither often available nor is it complete or consistent, even when given by experts. So, qualitative or semi-qualitative methods are likely to be alternatives.

He also recognized that a theory of belief revision requires a well-defined concept of conditionalisation, that is, it must assign conditional degrees of belief. He proposed modeling doxastic states by *Ordinal Conditional Functions*, though he now accepts the term *Ranking Functions* Spohn [1998].

Roughly speaking, Ranking Function is an ordered set of degrees over propositions, such that a proposition ϕ has rank κ if and only if $\kappa(\phi) = n$, where n is a non-negative integer.

Therefore, a ranking function κ maps each proposition ϕ, φ, ψ, ..., to a non-negative integer with at least one proposition having ranked 0. These integers are intended to represent *degrees of disbelief*, i.e., a proposition with rank 0 is not disbelieved at all, while a proposition with rank 1 is disbelieved to degree 1 and so on, as depicted on Figure 2.2.2.

In a disjunction of propositions, the belief degree is their minimal rank, for the reason that if one disbelieves a proposition to some degree, then one cannot have a greater disbelief in its disjunction. Formally:

$$\kappa(\phi \vee \psi) = \min(\kappa(\phi), \kappa(\psi))$$

If a proposition is conditioned to another, then the degree of disbelief is the rank of both propositions minus the rank of the conditioned one. Formally:

$\kappa(\phi) = 0$	ϕ and $\neg\phi$ are possible
$\kappa(\phi) = 1$	$\neg\phi$ is believed
$\kappa(\phi) = 2$	$\neg\phi$ is strongly believed
$\kappa(\phi) = 3$	$\neg\phi$ is very strongly believed
$\vdots$	$\vdots$

Figure 2.2   Ranking Function

$$\kappa(\phi \to \psi) = \kappa(\phi \wedge \psi) - \kappa(\phi)$$

These definitions form the *kappa calculus*. In fact, *kappa calculus* corresponds to an order of magnitude abstraction of (semi-qualitative) probability measures over propositions. The preference relation among conditionals in Spohn's Theory is then determined by the rank *kappa* of the model, such that the conditional $\phi \to \psi$ is preferred to $\phi \to \neg\psi$ if and only if $\kappa(\phi \to \psi) < \kappa(\phi \to \neg\psi)$.

Belief revision in Spohn's Theory corresponds to conditioning the ranking function with respect to some new relevant circumstance. For such conditionalization, Spohn provided a theory which allows a proposition to be shifted by some degree producing a new ranking function. This approach is related to Jeffrey's conditionalization for probability distribution Jeffrey [1965].

2.2.3 Some model-preference systems

We briefly describe some systems based on preferential relations among models.

2.2.3.1 ε-Semantics   The notion of ε-semantics goes back to Adams [1975].

A conditional knowledge base Δ is ε-consistent if and only if there exists a world ranking[7] that is admissible with respect to Δ. Otherwise, it is ε-inconsistent.

A conditional knowledge base Δ ε-entails a conditional $\phi \to \psi$, given a world ranking κ admissible with Δ, if and only if either $\kappa(\phi) = \infty$ (i.e., ϕ is unsatisfiable) or $\kappa(\phi \wedge \psi) < \kappa(\phi \wedge \neg\psi)$. Moreover, Δ *properly* ε-entails $\phi \to \psi$ if and only if Δ ε-entails $\phi \to \psi$ and Δ does not ε-entail $\phi \to \bot$.

2.2.3.2 Pearl's System Z   System Z was introduced by Pearl [1990] and its entailment applies to ε-consistent conditional knowledge bases $\Delta = (L, D)$, where L is the set of strict conditionals and D is the set of defeasible conditionals. D is z-partitioned in $D_0, ..., D_k$ such that each D_i, $0 \leq i < k$, is the set of all conditionals tolerated under L by $D - \bigcup\{D_j | 0 \leq j < i\}$. A conditional $\delta_m : \alpha \rightsquigarrow \beta$ is tolerated

---

[7] In this work, ε-Semantics are defined in terms of world ranking. For the equivalence to the original definitions, see Geffner (cf. Geffner [1992]).

by Δ iff $\{\alpha \wedge \beta\} \cup \Delta^* \not\models \bot$, where Δ^* is the material counterpart of Δ. The conditional δ has ranking j, for $0 \leq j < k$, iff $\delta \in D_j$. The ranking function $\kappa^z(w)$ on interpretations induced by Z is defined as follows:

$$k^z(w) = \begin{cases} \infty & \text{iff } w \not\models L \\ 0 & \text{iff } w \models L \cup D \\ 1 + \max_{\delta_m \in D_i : w \not\models \delta_m} Z(\delta_m) & \text{otherwise} \end{cases} \qquad (2.8)$$

A conditional $\phi \to \psi$ is z-entailed by Δ iff either $\kappa^z(\phi) = \infty$ or $\kappa^z(\phi \wedge \psi) < \kappa^z(\phi \wedge \neg\psi)$.

This semantics will be more detailed in the next Chapter.

2.2.3.3 Goldszmidt and Pearl's System Z^+

System Z^+ was introduced by Goldszmidt and Pearl [1991b] and it also applies to ε-consistent conditional knowledge bases Δ, however with defaults enriched by strength assignment σ. The concept of default ranking z^+ and world ranking κ^+ are in the core of the notion of z^+-entailment, and are defined as follows, for all $\delta = \phi \to \psi$:

$$z^+(\delta) = \sigma(\delta) + \kappa^+(\phi \wedge \psi) \qquad (2.9)$$

$$k^+(w) = \begin{cases} \infty & \text{iff } w \not\models L \\ 0 & \text{iff } w \models L \cup D \\ 1 + \max_{\delta_m \in D_i : w \not\models \delta_m} Z^+(\delta_m) & \text{otherwise} \end{cases} \qquad (2.10)$$

A conditional $\delta : \phi \to \psi$ is z^+-entailed by (Δ, σ) at strength τ iff either $\kappa^+(\phi) = \infty$ or $\kappa^+(\phi \wedge \psi) + \tau < \kappa^+(\phi \wedge \neg\psi)$.

Notice that for any $\Delta = (L, D)$ and for all $\delta \in D$, the default ranking z and the world ranking k^z coincide with z^+ and k^+ for Δ under strength assignment $\sigma(\delta) = 0$.

2.2.3.4 Pearl's Maximum Entropy

The notion of entailment in the Maximum Entropy approach of Goldszmidt *et al.* [1993] applies to ε-consistent conditional knowledge bases $\Delta = (L, D)$, where Δ is *minimal-core*, that is, for each default $\delta \in D$ there is a model w of $L \cup (D - \{\delta\})$ that falsifies δ. z^*-entailment is linked to a default ranking z^* and a world ranking k^*, which are defined as the following system of equations:

$$z^*(\delta) = 1 + \kappa^*(\phi \wedge \psi) \qquad (2.11)$$

$$k^*(w) = \begin{cases} \infty & \text{iff } w \not\models L \\ 0 & \text{iff } w \models L \cup D \\ \sum_{\delta_m \in D_i : w \not\models \delta_m} Z^*(\delta_m) & \text{otherwise} \end{cases} \qquad (2.12)$$

A default $\delta : \phi \to \psi$ is z^*-entailed by Δ iff either $\kappa^*(\phi) = \infty$ or $\kappa^*(\phi \wedge \psi) < \kappa^*(\phi \wedge \neg\psi)$.

2.2.3.5 Bourne and Parsons' Maximum Entropy with Variable Strength Defaults

Bourne and Parsons (Bourne and Parsons [1999], Bourne [1999]) extended Maximum Entropy Semantics to variable strength defaults, and the $z_s^\star$-entailment is a proper generalization of $z^\star$-entailment. This approach applies to ε-consistent conditional knowledge bases $\Delta = (L, D)$ with positive strength assignments σ and $z_s^\star$-entailment is based on the following system of equations with positive $z_s^\star$, for all $\delta : \phi \to \psi$:

$$k_s^\star(\phi \wedge \neg\psi) = \sigma(\phi \to \psi) + \kappa_s^\star(\phi \wedge \psi) \tag{2.13}$$

$$k_s^\star(w) = \begin{cases} \infty & \text{iff } w \not\models L \\ 0 & \text{iff } w \models L \cup D \\ \displaystyle\sum_{\delta_m \in D_i : w \not\models \delta_m} Z_s^\star(\delta_m) & \text{otherwise} \end{cases} \tag{2.14}$$

$\Delta = (L, D)$ is said to be *robust* iff $z_s^\star$ and $\kappa_s^\star$ has a unique solution, such that $z_s^\star$ is positive and $\kappa_s^\star$ is robust. $\kappa_s^\star$ is *robust* iff for all distinct defaults δ_1 and δ_2 in D, it holds that all models w_1 and w_2 of L having smallest ranking in $\kappa_s^\star$ such that $w_1 \not\models \delta_1$ and $w_2 \not\models \delta_2$, respectively, are different. In other words, δ_1 and δ_2 do not have a common minimal falsifying model under L.

A default $\delta : \phi \to \psi$ is $z_s^\star$-entailed by (Δ, σ) at strength τ iff either $\kappa_s^\star(\phi) = \infty$ or $\kappa_s^\star(\phi \wedge \psi) + \tau \le \kappa_s^\star(\phi \wedge \neg\psi)$.

2.2.3.6 Benferhat et al's Lexicographic Entailment

Benferhat et al's Lexicographic Entailment Benferhat *et al.* [1993] applies to conditional knowledge bases $\Delta = (L, D)$ that are not necessarily ε-consistent. The conditional knowledge base Δ has a priority assignment π, which defines an ordered partition $(D_0, ..., D_k)$ of D by $D_i = \{\delta \in D : \pi(\delta) = i\}$, for all $i \le k$. A *preference ordering* on worlds is defined such that a world w is π-preferable to a word w' iff there exists some $i \in \{0, ..., k\}$ such that $|\{\delta \in D_i : w \models \delta\}| > |\{\delta \in D_i : w' \models \delta\}|$ and $|\{\delta \in D_j : w \models \delta\}| = |\{\delta \in D_j : w' \models \delta\}|$ for all $i < j \le k$. Expressed in terms of world ranking, we say that a model w of a set of classical formulas $\mathcal{F}$ is a π-preferred model of $\mathcal{F}$ iff no model of $\mathcal{F}$ is π-preferable to w.

A conditional $\delta : \phi \to \psi$ is lex_p-entailed by (Δ, π) iff ψ is satisfied in every π-preferred model of $L \cup \{\phi\}$.

2.2.3.7 Lehmann's Lexicographic Closure

The Lexicographic Closure introduced by Lehmann [1995] is a special case of the lexicographic entailment of Benferhat *et al.* [1993]. The Lexicographic Closure of Lehmann [1995] uses the default ranking z of Δ as a particular priority assignment which is logically entrenched in Δ. Hence, Δ is ε-consistent since the priority assignment π coincides with the default ranking z of Δ.

A default $\delta : \phi \to \psi$ is *lex*-entailed by Δ iff $\delta : \phi \to \psi$ is lex_p-entailed by (Δ, z). This semantics will be more detailed in the next chapter.

2.2.3.8 *Geffner's Conditional Entailment*   The Conditional Entailment approach was introduced by Geffner [1992], and it applies to conditional knowledge bases $\Delta = (L, D)$ with an irreflexive and transitive binary *priority ordering* relation $\prec$ on D. Δ is *conditionally consistent* iff there exists an admissible priority relation $\prec$ on D with respect to Δ. Remark that, according to Eiter and Lukasiewicz [2000], the notion of ε-consistency coincides with the notion of conditional consistency.

We say that $\prec$ is *admissible* with respect to Δ iff each set of defaults $D' \subseteq D$ that is under L in conflict with some default $\delta \in D$ contains a default δ' such that $\delta' \prec \delta$. Next, we define a *preference ordering* on worlds based on $\prec$. A world w is $\prec$-preferable to a world w', denoted by $w \prec w'$, iff $\{\delta \in D : w \not\models \delta\} \neq \{\delta \in D : w' \not\models \delta\}$ and for each default $\delta \in D$ such that $w \not\models \delta$ and $w' \models \delta$, there exists a default $\delta' \in D$ such that $\delta \prec \delta'$, $w \models \delta'$ and $w' \not\models \delta'$. A model w of a set of classical formulas $\mathcal{F}$ is a $\prec$-preferred model of $\mathcal{F}$ iff no model of $\mathcal{F}$ is $\prec$-preferable to w.

A conditional $\delta : \phi \rightarrow \psi$ is *conditionally entailed* by Δ iff ψ is satisfied in every $\prec$-preferred model of $L \cup \{\phi\}$ of every priority ordering $\prec$ that is admissible with respect to Δ.

CHAPTER 3

CONDITIONAL LOGICS AND LEGAL REASONING

Τὸν ηττω λόγον κρείττω ποιεῖε
(Changing the argumentation from the weakest to the strongest)

—Protágoras, A 21, B 6b D.-K.

3.1 Semantics for Legal Reasoning

This Chapter presents the logical framework that will be used in this dissertation to model legal reasoning and also its respective translation. The semantics are presented in their original format and then will be extended to yield the reasoning structure that characterizes the inference in law.

3.1.1 Language and Notation

In the present work, I shall mainly use the propositional calculus language. One should assume that $\mathcal{P}$ is the propositional alphabet of a finite language $\mathcal{L}$. The $\mathcal{P}$ set is enriched with two symbols $\top$ (logical truthfulness) and $\bot$ (logical falsity). One should assume also that propositional formulas, denoted by Greek letters $\alpha, \psi, \phi, \dots$

are built inductively by using the propositional letters existing in $\mathcal{P}$, and logical connectives. Symbol $\models$ represents logical consequence and $\vdash$ means logical provability. An *interpretation* is an assignment of "true" or "false" to every *propositional letters* $a_1, \ldots, a_j, \ldots, a_n$. An interpretation of $\mathcal{L}$ is a function w of $\mathcal{P}$ to boolean values $\{\top, \bot\}$. This function can be extended to propositions built from the alphabet $\mathcal{P}$ in the usual way, such that $w(\alpha \wedge \beta) = \top$ iff $w(\alpha) = \top$ and $w(\beta) = \top$, etc. $\mathcal{W}$ represents the set of all possible interpretations. A model for a set of propositions H is an interpretation w such that $w(\alpha) = \top$ for all $\alpha \in H$.

Technically, the conditional knowledge base Δ will be represented by means of a pair (D, L), where L is a finite set of extreme conditionals, written as: $\alpha_i \Rightarrow \beta_i$, and D is a finite set of defeasible conditionals, written as: $\alpha_i \rightarrow \beta_i$. Each sentence $\alpha_i \Rightarrow \beta_i$ is interpreted as "If α_i then definitely β_i ", while each sentence $\alpha_i \rightarrow \beta_i$ is interpreted as "If α_i then normally / typically β_i". Both $\Rightarrow$ and $\rightarrow$ are meta-connectives, where $\Rightarrow$ means definitely and $\rightarrow$ means normally / typically, which can occur only as the main connective. The difference among strict and defeasible conditionals may not be clear in the legal context by now, but I shall return to this issue in section 1.3.1. We will refer to a rule on Δ that can be either strict or defeasible as a *conditional* sentence δ. The conditional rule with antecedent α_i and consequent β_i has the *material counterpart* by replacing the connective by the material implication[1] connective $\supset$, denoted by $\alpha_i \supset \beta_i$, and the material counterpart of Δ will be represented by Δ^*. Besides, an interpretation w satisfies a conditional δ, or it is a model of δ, denoted by $w \models \delta$, iff $w \models \alpha \supset \beta$, i.e., iff w satisfies the material counterpart of δ. An interpretation w satisfies a set Δ of strict and defeasible rules, or w is a model of Δ, denoted by $w \models \Delta$, iff w satisfies each member of Δ. An interpretation w verifies a conditional δ, denoted by $w \models \delta$, iff $w \models \alpha \wedge \beta$. Furthermore, w falsifies a conditional δ iff $w \models \alpha \wedge \neg \beta$.

3.1.2 System Z

First let us take a running example which will be used throughout this chapter to explain the semantics for legal reasoning. In tort law, trespass (to land or to chattels) describes the interference with the right to possession, and such kind of tort entitles a claim for compensation for environmental damage. The actor is liable for all consequences of his actions, and intentional trespass does not limit liability to foreseeable damages, as occurs in liability for negligence. Nevertheless, liability could be excluded as the result of the express or implied consent by the plaintiff, or in case of public necessity. This set of observations can be represented in the following conditional knowledge base:

■ **EXAMPLE 3.1**

---

[1]In this work we distinguish $\alpha \Rightarrow \beta$ and $\alpha \supset \beta$, where the former denotes generic knowledge and the later an item of evidence. For a complete discussion, see Goldszmidt and Pearl [1991a].

[Trespass and Liability] Consider the following legal knowledge base, regarding to tort cases:

$$\Delta = \begin{cases} \delta_1 : t \to l \\ \delta_2 : t \to ed \\ \delta_3 : c \to t \\ \delta_4 : c \to \neg l \end{cases} \tag{3.1}$$

Rules δ_i represent the following situations: $[\delta_1]$ a trespass (t) normally entitles a claim for liability (l) of the actor and $[\delta_2]$ normally causes an environmental damage (ed); however $[\delta_3]$ the actor may have an express or implied consent (c) from the plaintiff to trespass (t), and $[\delta_4]$ the consent (c) excludes the liability $(\neg l)$.

From the description of Δ we use the specificity relations among the defeasible legal norms in order to establish preference relations between the interpretations that a (legal) agent foresees as possible. The determination of the specificity relations is made using system Z Pearl [1990], which defines a unique partition of the set of defeasible sentences D, into ordered sets of mutually exclusive defeasible sentences $D_0, D_1, ..., D_n$.

The notion of tolerance is the main concept used to determine this partitioning. A rule is tolerated by Δ if the antecedent and the consequent of this rule are not in direct conflict with any inference sanctioned by Δ^*, where Δ^* is the material counterpart of Δ.

Definition 25 (Tolerance) *Pearl [1990] A conditional δ_i with antecedent α and consequent β is tolerated by a conditional set Δ iff $\{\alpha \wedge \beta\} \cup \Delta^* \not\models \bot$.*

Using tolerance, Pearl [1990] developed a syntactical test for consistency that generates the partition of a conditional knowledge base and, hence, the ranking among defeasible rules.

Definition 26 *Pearl [1990] D is p-consistent iff we can build an ordered partition of $D = (D_0, ..., D_n)$ where:*
1. each conditional in D_i, $1 \leq i \leq n$, is tolerated by $L \cup (D - \bigcup \{D_j | 0 \leq j < i\})$.
2. every conditional in L is tolerated by L.

The partition of $D = (D_0, ..., D_n)$ has the following property: Every defeasible legal norm belonging to D_i is tolerated by $L \cup \bigcup_{j=i}^{n} D_j$, where n is the number of the subsets in the partition. Notice that there is no partition of L. A strict legal norm cannot be overruled but only defeasible ones can. For this reason, the set of strict legal norms L are excluded from the partitioning. We shall see an example with strict rules in Section 3.3.1.

The strength of a legal norm is its Z-rank such that to each legal norm δ_i in Δ is assigned a Z-rank equal to the index of that partition set to which it belongs:

w_i	t	l	c	ed	k^z
w_1	F	F	F	F	0
w_2	F	F	F	T	0
w_3	F	F	T	F	2
w_4	F	F	T	T	2
w_5	F	T	F	F	0
w_6	F	T	F	T	0
w_7	F	T	T	F	2
w_8	F	T	T	T	2

w_i	t	l	c	ed	k^z
w_9	T	F	F	F	1
w_{10}	T	F	F	T	1
w_{11}	T	F	T	F	1
w_{12}	T	F	T	T	1
w_{13}	T	T	F	F	1
w_{14}	T	T	F	T	0
w_{15}	T	T	T	F	2
w_{16}	T	T	T	T	2

Figure 3.1   The Ranking $k^z(w_i)$ for the trespass example.

Definition 27 (Strength of a legal norm) *Let $Z(\delta_m)$ be the strength of the legal norm δ_m, then*

$$Z(\delta_m) = \begin{cases} i & \text{iff } \delta_m \in D_i \\ \infty & \text{iff } \delta_m \in L \end{cases}$$

Definition 28 (Order relation among legal norms) *A defeasible legal norm δ_i has greater strength than δ_j if and only if $Z(\delta_j) < Z(\delta_i)$.*

■ **EXAMPLE 3.2**

Example (3.1) yields the following partition of D:

$$D_0 = \{\delta_1, \delta_2\} \text{ and } D_1 = \{\delta_3, \delta_4\}$$

Hence, the strength of the legal norms, $Z(\delta_i)$, are:

$$Z(\delta_1) = Z(\delta_2) = 0 \text{ and } Z(\delta_3) = Z(\delta_4) = 1$$

The ranking function $\kappa^z(w)$ on interpretations induced by Z is defined as follows:

$$k^z(w) = \begin{cases} \infty & \text{iff } w \not\models L \\ 0 & \text{iff } w \models L \cup D \\ 1 + \max\limits_{\delta_m \in D_i : w \not\models \delta_m} Z(\delta_m) & \text{otherwise} \end{cases} \qquad (3.2)$$

A conditional $\delta_i : \phi \to \psi$ is z-entailed by Δ iff either $\kappa^z(\phi) = \infty$ or $\kappa^z(\phi \wedge \psi) < \kappa_z(\phi \wedge \neg\psi)$.

▣ EXAMPLE 3.3

In example 3.1, $\mathcal{L}$ has four atoms and thus $\mathcal{W}$ has 2^4 models. These models are depicted in Figure (3.2) along with their $\kappa^z(w)$. Thus, example 3.1 yields the following possible inferences under System Z. Initially, let us see whether the conditional "a trespass (t) to land (ln) causing an environmental damage (ed) entitles a claim for liability (l)" $(t \wedge ln \wedge ed \rightarrow l)$ is z-entailed or not. The proposition ln is added to $\mathcal{L}$, however it has no effect on the κ^z-ranks of the models:

$$\kappa^z(t \wedge ln \wedge ed \wedge l) = 0 < 1 = \kappa^z(t \wedge ln \wedge ed \wedge \neg l)$$

Hence, the conditional augmented with ln is z-entailed (such as the conditional $t \wedge \neg ln \rightarrow l$). Since ln are referred to by no conditional in Δ, it is irrelevant to the consequence relation. System Z adequately disregards the irrelevant proposition, if such is a property of a general class. Nevertheless, System Z fails to inherit a property to an exceptional subclass. Let us take now the conditional "the consent (c) to the actor caused an environment damage (ed)". In this case, $c \rightarrow ed$ is not z-entailed:

$$\kappa^z(c \wedge ed) = 1 = \kappa^z(c \wedge \neg ed)$$

Since the conditional $t \rightarrow ed$ has the same z-rank of $t \rightarrow l$, which is falsified by the consent $(c \rightarrow \neg l)$, System Z cannot see the abnormality of the consent yielding or not an environment damage and hence does not sanction property inheritance to exceptional subclasses.

The consequence relation should include not only property inheritance of the same class, but exceptional subclasses should also inherit it from general classes. To capture this feature, the semantics will be refined to the lexicographic closure.

3.1.3 Lexicographic Closure

The Lexicographic Closure as introduced by Lehmann [1995] holds the assumption that the consequence relation should satisfy four presumptions: typicality, independence, priority and specificity. Lehmann noticed in (Lehmann and Magidor [1992]) that all conditionals are presumed to be active unless there is direct evidence against it. However, there are situations where not all conditionals can be active at the same time. Thus, he proposes a lexicographical ordering, keeping the priorities relations given by Pearl [1990]'s System Z, and then offering a second criterion.

In the first place, the lexicographical ordering assumes a natural ordering of conditionals, given by its specificity relation, such that it is more serious to falsify the conditionals belonging to a higher rank than those conditionals with lower rank. When both conditionals have the same level, the second criterion is used. Upon it, the lexicographical ordering assumes that, *all-else-being-equal*, it is worse to falsify more conditionals at the same rank, so that an interpretation that falsifies less conditionals *all-else-being-equal* is preferred to those that falsifies more conditionals.

Therefore, the Lexicographic Closure defined by Lehmann [1995] is a modular ordering, M_d, under the interpretations that belong to W. Each interpretation is ordered according to the ranking of the set of defeasible conditional it falsifies, such that each interpretation m falsifies a set $\overline{D}_m \subseteq D$ of defaults. The lexicographic entailment prefers the interpretations that falsifies a "lighter" set of defeasible rules, i.e. an interpretation that falsifies a "lighter" set of defaults is more normal than a model that falsifies a more "serious" one. According to Lehmann two criteria should be taken into account when comparing the interpretations:

1. the specificity of the falsified defeasible sentences by each interpretation: an interpretation that falsifies a less specific defeasible rule is preferred to an interpretation that falsifies a more specific one.

2. the size of the set falsified by each interpretation: the smaller the set, the more preferred is the interpretation. "Smaller" in the sense of size of the set, i.e., its cardinality, not by set inclusion.

In situations when these two criteria will be in conflict, a rational agent should prefer a criterion rather than the other. The lexicographic entailment chooses to favor the specificity. Thus, the rational agent should prefer to falsify two defeasible sentences less specific than a more specific one.

Definition 29 *Lehmann [1995] Assume that $D_0, D_1, ..., D_n$ is the partitioning of D. Suppose also that w is an interpretation and $\overline{D}_w$ is the set of defaults falsified by w. $v_i(w)$ represents the number of defaults belonging to partition D_i falsified by interpretation w, i.e., $v_i(w) = |D_i \cap \overline{D}_w|$.*

Thus, each interpretation w can be associated to a tuple of $n+1$ natural numbers: $\langle v_n(w), \ldots, v_0(w) \rangle$

Definition 30 (Lexicographic ordering) *Lehmann [1995] An interpretation w_p is preferred with respect to an interpretation w_q, denoted by $w_p \prec w_q$, iff $\langle v_n(w_p), \ldots, v_0(w_p) \rangle < \langle v_n(w_q), \ldots, v_0(w_q) \rangle$, where $<$ is a lexicographic ordering under natural numbers.*

Definition 31 *An interpretation w_p is a minimal interpretation wrt lexicographic ordering iff there is no w_q such that $w_q \prec w_p$, i.e., iff there is no interpretation that is preferred to w_p wrt lexicographic ordering.*

Definition 32 (Lexicographic entailment) *A defeasible conditional $\alpha \to \beta$ is lexicographically entailed by Δ, $\Delta|\!\sim_{lex} \alpha \to \beta$, iff all preferred interpretation wrt lexicographic ordering that satisfies α also satisfies β.*

■ **EXAMPLE 3.4**

Given the set of legal conditionals Δ of example 3.1, and its z-partition in $D_0 = \{\delta_1, \delta_2\} \cup D_1 = \{\delta_3, \delta_4\}$, a 2-tuple is assigned to each model, with

w_i	t	l	c	ed	Lex
w_1	F	F	F	F	$\langle 0,0 \rangle$
w_2	F	F	F	T	$\langle 0,0 \rangle$
w_3	F	F	T	F	$\langle 1,0 \rangle$
w_4	F	F	T	T	$\langle 1,0 \rangle$
w_5	F	T	F	F	$\langle 0,0 \rangle$
w_6	F	T	F	T	$\langle 0,0 \rangle$
w_7	F	T	T	F	$\langle 2,0 \rangle$
w_8	F	T	T	T	$\langle 2,0 \rangle$

w_i	t	l	c	ed	Lex
w_9	T	F	F	F	$\langle 0,2 \rangle$
w_{10}	T	F	F	T	$\langle 0,1 \rangle$
w_{11}	T	F	T	F	$\langle 0,2 \rangle$
w_{12}	T	F	T	T	$\langle 0,1 \rangle$
w_{13}	T	T	F	F	$\langle 0,1 \rangle$
w_{14}	T	T	F	T	$\langle 0,0 \rangle$
w_{15}	T	T	T	F	$\langle 1,1 \rangle$
w_{16}	T	T	T	T	$\langle 1,0 \rangle$

Figure 3.2 The *Lex*-tuples for the trespass example.

the number of conditionals it violates in the position i of the partition D_i. In Example 3.1, we assign to the first position of the tuple (from right to left) the number of conditionals falsified in the partition D_i and, then, we assign to the next position of the tuple the number of conditionals falsified in the partition D_{i+1} yielding the lexicographical ordering depicted in Figure 3.1.3. If one tuple has fewer conditional violations in the highest tuple element (from left to right), it is preferred in the Lexicographical Closure. The legal norm "the consent caused an environment damage" is *lex*-entailed if it is preferred by the minimal verifying and falsifying models of $c \to ed$. According to the lexicographic closure of Δ:

$$lex(c \wedge ed) = \langle 0, 1 \rangle < \langle 0, 2 \rangle = lex(c \wedge \neg ed)$$

that is, $w_{12} \prec w_{11}$.

Therefore, $c \to ed$ is *lex*-entailed and lexicographical ordering can handle with inheritance to exceptional subclasses.

Notice that lexicographical closure is a direct extension of System Z and it corresponds to the rational consequence relation, being a total ordering over models, as such. Thus, lexicographical closure can sanction property inheritance, specificity and indifference as in System Z. Moreover, it can also sanction exceptional inheritance, since it yields a consequence relation by comparing the number and the degree of conditional violations.

3.2 Extending the Semantics

In lexicographical closure, *any number* of lower rank conditionals is preferred to a single higher rank one. Some authors claim that this feature is not quite accurate when we need no longer accepting the stronger conditional in favor of a larger number of weaker ones. According to [Bourne, 1999, pp. 51 ff.]:

While one can argue that some defaults may have priority over others, it is hard to justify some as having infinite priority over others so that any number of lower violations are better than a single higher one. There may come a point when it seems more reasonable to abandon accepting the stronger default in favour of accepting a larger number of weaker ones. In terms of the penguin example, it may be more reasonable to reject the belief that a penguin is a bird when it displays no bird attributes rather than insisting that it is bird which exhibits none of them. Under LEX-entailment, this kind of weighing up of default violations cannot occur, and there is no room for such refinements of judgement, since the priorities are fixed by the z-partition and the chosen method of ordering LEX-tuples.

The observation of Bourne is very interesting. It shows an important feature for legal reasoning: The possibility of cumulating reasons, enhancing the strength of an outcome (see section 1.4.2 of Chapter 1).

However, it is very controversial whether *conditionals* should cumulate or not. In legal reasoning, one cannot say that an outcome is stronger because a certain legal system has *two* or more statutory rules (at the same level, i.e., not in chain) for that outcome. Even if one accepts that rules can be weighed, it does not mean that a rule will be stronger when cumulated with another rule, if both rules are not in chain. For a distinction between *cumulating-and-chain* and *chain-without-cumulating*, see Peczenik [1997a].

Actually, what should accumulate are reasons, without the if-then structure, like observations, evidence, principles, values and so forth. When a rule is weighed, it belongs to a chain that forms the argument. So, the argument will be weighed against other arguments. A rule may accumulate with another reasons, to make the outcome stronger. In this case, we are not combining two rules, but the outcome of the rule and an information without the if-then structure. Hence, if-then rules should not accumulate[2].

This feature is emphasized by [Goldszmidt and Pearl, 1996, pp. 78]. They write:

> First, in many systems it is convenient to treat if-then rules as a stable part of our knowledge, unperturbed by observations made about a particular individual or in any specific set of circumstances. This permits us to compile rules into a structure that allows efficient processing over a long stream of queries. Adding query-induced rules to the knowledge base will neutralize this facility.
>
> Second, rules and observations combine differently: The latter should accumulate, the former do not. For example, if we have two rules $a \xrightarrow{\delta_1} c$ and $b \xrightarrow{\delta_2} c$ and we observe a and b, system-Z^+ would believe c to a degree $\max(\delta_1, \delta_2)$. However, if a and b provide two independent reasons for believing c, the two observations together should endow c with a belief that is stronger than any one component in isolation.

The accrual of reasons is an important characteristic of legal reasoning. In certain situations one may either have only indirect evidence for the consequence or the legal norms are too vague (soft) and need a different strength attribution. As we have

---

[2]Notice that the formalism of maximum entropy embodies the conditional independence among converging rules

seen in Section 1.4.2 of Chapter 1, in the *accrual of reasons*, some reasons which individually are outweighed by other reasons due to an absolute priority relation, together may 'weigh' more than the reason which initially was stronger. Therefore, in the case of merely indirect (or 'soft') reasons for the conclusion, they should accumulate, since several reasons considered together may outweigh another reason, as long as the former reason is not taken separately.

Consequently, we need a slight refinement of the lexicographic semantics for modeling legal reasoning in conditional logics and assigning a variable degree of strength to conditionals are likely to be a viable alternative. This will be investigated in the following sections.

3.2.1 Variable Strength Conditionals

Variable strength conditionals provide the user with the power to explicitly set a weight for conditionals. The specification of a conditional should be extended with a parameter representing the *'degree of strength'* or *'firmness'* of the conditional.

Since we need an explicit assignment of the strength of conditionals, Benferhat *et al*'s Lexicographic entailment would be an attractive semantics. Recall that the system introduced by Benferhat *et al.* [1993] applies to Conditional Knowledge Bases that are ε-inconsistent, that is, without the priority ordering of System Z. The conditional knowledge base Δ has a priority assignment π, assigned by the user which defines a partitioning of D in $(D_0, ..., D_k)$ such that $D_i = \{\delta \in D : \pi(\delta) = i\}$, for all $i \leq k$. Lexicographical ordering of Benferhat *et al.* [1993] is a generalization of Lexicographic Closure of Lehmann [1995].

Nevertheless, it is desirable to keep the properties of Lehmann's Lexicographic Closure. However, it is also desired a system which is flexible enough to support conditionals with variable strength. Thus, we need a system that fluctuates between Lehmann's lexicographic closure and Benferhat's lexicographical ordering.

For such account, I shall introduce an extension of Lehmann's Lexicographic Closure. Such extension can be obtained by an assignment of variable strength to the conditionals, though retaining the main properties of System Z, as was proposed in System Z^+ by Goldszmidt and Pearl in Goldszmidt and Pearl [1991b] and in Goldszmidt and Pearl [1996]. This System shall be explained in the next Section.

3.2.2 System Z^+ and ε-consistent Knowledge Bases

System Z^+ was introduced by Goldszmidt and Pearl, altogether with the notion of variable strength defaults. It also applies to ε-consistent conditional knowledge bases Δ, however with defaults enriched by strength assignment σ. Variable strength rules extend the specification of $\delta_i : \phi_i \rightarrow \psi_i$ with a nonnegative integer assigned as a parameter σ_i, denoted by $\delta_i : \phi_i \xrightarrow{\sigma_i} \psi_i$, representing the *"degree of strength or firmness"* of the conditional. Notice that after the assignment of the extra strength attribute, the main properties of the *flat* system, that is, System Z, are retained.

Definition 33 *[Goldszmidt and Pearl, 1996, p.70] Given a set of variable strength conditionals, denoted by $\Delta^+ = \{\delta_i | \delta_i : \phi_i \xrightarrow{\sigma_i} \psi_i, 1 \leq i \leq n\}$, where $|\Delta^+| = n$, a ranking κ is admissible with respect to Δ^+, iff*

$$\kappa(\phi_i \wedge \psi_i) < \sigma_i + \kappa(\phi_i \wedge \neg\psi_i) \tag{3.3}$$

Hence, a conditional knowledge base Δ^+ is consistent iff there exists an admissible ranking κ with respect to Δ^+. The definition 33 is equivalent to $\kappa(\neg\psi_i | \phi_i) > \sigma_i$, for every conditional $\phi_i \xrightarrow{\sigma_i} \psi_i \in \Delta^+$ Goldszmidt and Pearl [1996]. According to a theorem of Goldszmidt and Pearl (cf. Goldszmidt and Pearl [1996]), Δ^+ is consistent iff Δ is consistent.

The definition of Z^+ is given by the concept of default ranking Z^+ and world ranking κ^+, as follows:

$$Z^+(\delta) = min\{\kappa^+(w) | w \models \phi_i \wedge \psi_i\} + \sigma_i \tag{3.4}$$

$$k^+(w) = \begin{cases} \infty & \text{iff } w \not\models L \\ 0 & \text{iff } w \models L \cup D \\ 1 + \max_{\delta_m \in D_i : w \not\models \delta_m} Z^+(\delta_m) & \text{otherwise} \end{cases} \tag{3.5}$$

The procedure for ordering variable strength defaults in System Z^+ System is given by the following algorithm.

Algorithm for Z^+ ordering
Input: A consistent knowledge base Δ^+.
Output: Z^+-ordering on rules.

1. Let Δ_0 be the set of rules tolerated by Δ^+, and let RZ^+ be an empty set.

2. For each rule $\delta_i : \phi_i \xrightarrow{\sigma_i} \psi_i \in \Delta_0$, set $Z(\delta_i) = \sigma_i$ and $RZ^+ = RZ^+ \cup \{\delta_i\}$.

3. While $RZ^+ \neq \Delta^+$, do:

   (a) Let $\Delta^\star$ be the set of rules in $\Delta' = \Delta^+ - RZ^+$ tolerated by Δ'.

   (b) For each $\delta : \phi \xrightarrow{\sigma} \varphi \in \Delta^\star$, let Ω_δ denote the set of models for $\phi \wedge \varphi$ that do not violate any rule in Δ'; compute

   $$Z(\delta) = \min_{w_\delta \in \Omega_\delta} [\kappa(w_\delta)] + \sigma \tag{3.6}$$

   where

   $$\kappa(w_\delta) = \max_{\delta_j \in RZ^+} \{Z(\delta_j) | w_\delta \models \phi_j \wedge \neg\psi_j\} + 1 \tag{3.7}$$

   and $\delta_j : \phi_j \xrightarrow{\sigma_j} \psi_j \in RZ^+$.

   (c) Let $\delta^\star$ be a rule in $\Delta^\star$ having the lowest Z; set $RZ^+ = RZ^+ \cup \{\delta^\star\}$.

Although it may appear that $Z(\delta)$ is defined by $\kappa(w_\delta)$ and $\kappa(w_\delta)$ is defined by $Z(\delta)$, this definition is not recursive, since it will always be based on the rank of last partition.

w_i	t	l	c	ed	z^+
w_1	F	F	F	F	0
w_2	F	F	F	T	0
w_3	F	F	T	F	4
w_4	F	F	T	T	4
w_5	F	T	F	F	0
w_6	F	T	F	T	0
w_7	F	T	T	F	4
w_8	F	T	T	T	4

w_i	t	l	c	ed	z^+
w_9	T	F	F	F	3
w_{10}	T	F	F	T	2
w_{11}	T	F	T	F	3
w_{12}	T	F	T	T	2
w_{13}	T	T	F	F	3
w_{14}	T	T	F	T	0
w_{15}	T	T	T	F	4
w_{16}	T	T	T	T	4

Figure 3.3   The Ranking $k^+(w_i)$ for the trespass example.

Once Z^+ of each default and the rank κ^+ of each interpretation are known, we can establish the entailment under the consequence relation induced by κ^+.

A conditional $\delta : \phi_i \xrightarrow{\sigma_i} \psi_i$ is z^+-entailed by Δ^+ at strength τ iff either $\kappa^+(\phi) = \infty$ or $\kappa^+(\phi \wedge \psi) + \tau < \kappa^+(\phi \wedge \neg\psi)$.

Notice that for any $\Delta = (L, D)$ and for all $\delta_i \in D$, the default ranking z and the world ranking k^z coincide with z^+ and k^+ for Δ under strength assignment $\sigma(\delta_i) = 0$.

◼ EXAMPLE 3.5

[Trespass and Liability augmented] Consider the Example 3.1 augmented by a strength assignment σ_i:

$$\Delta^+ = \begin{cases} \delta_1 : t \xrightarrow{1} l \\ \delta_2 : t \xrightarrow{2} ed \\ \delta_3 : c \xrightarrow{1} t \\ \delta_4 : c \xrightarrow{1} \neg l \end{cases} \tag{3.8}$$

The knowledge base Δ^+ is Z^+-ordered as follows: Since both δ_1 and δ_2 are tolerated by all the rules in the knowledge base, $Z^+(\delta_1) = \sigma_1 = 1$ and $Z^+(\delta_2) = \sigma_2 = 2$. Any κ^+-minimal world verifying δ_3 and δ_4 must falsify δ_1. Hence, according to Z^+-ordering, $Z^+(\delta_3) = \sigma_1 + \sigma_3 + 1 = 3$ and $Z^+(\delta_4) = \sigma_1 + \sigma_4 + 1 = 3$. The models w_i are depicted in Figure 3.5. We can see that the conditional "the consent caused an environmental damage" is z^+-entailed:

$$z^+(c \wedge ed) = 2 < 3 = z^+(c \wedge \neg ed)$$

Thus, enhancing the strength of certain conditionals allows some desirable inferences. In this example, inheritance to exceptional subclasses was obtained. This approach has shortcomings. Such solution does not seem to be the best one to handle the exceptional inheritance, since it should be satisfied independently of any strength assignment, just as in the lexicographical ordering. However, the assignment of an explicit strength to a certain rule is very useful, which encourages the use of variable strength conditionals.

3.2.3   A New Semantics: System Lex^+

In Lehmann's Lexicographical Closure, the priority relation is given by System Z respecting the specificity, and then the number of falsified conditionals is confronted in a certain partition, whilst in Bernferhat *et al.*'s approach the priority is leaved up to the user. I shall call Lex^+ the semantics that fluctuate between Lehmann's work and Benferhat's approach. The main idea behind Lex^+ semantics is to enhance the Lehmann's Lexicographic Ordering with variable strength conditionals, however, keeping the ε-consistency of the knowledge base.

Definition 34 (Admissible Ranking) *A ranking κ is admissible with respect to Δ^+ iff*

$$\kappa(\phi_i \wedge \psi_i) < \sigma_i + \kappa(\phi_i \wedge \neg\psi_i) \tag{3.9}$$

Definition 35 (Lex^+-Consistency) *A conditional knowledge base Δ^+ is consistent iff there exists an admissible ranking κ with respect to Δ^+.*

The partitioning of a conditional knowledge base Δ^+ is the central component in establishing consistency and also the priorities among defaults. Thus, we must specify the partition of Δ^+. To augment the lexicographical ordering with variable strength conditionals, it is necessary to generate a partition distinctive from System Z, now considering the parameter of strength assigned to each conditional.

Definition 36 (Partitioning of Knowledge Base) *A knowledge base $\Delta^+ = (L, D)$ is partitioned into $D = (D_0, D_1, ..., D_n)$ under a priority assignment π such that $D_i = \{\delta \in D : \pi(\delta) = i\}$, for all $i \leq n$.*

Now, we shall define the priority relation π which gives the ordering over D. This priority among conditionals is given by the Z^+-ordering of Goldszmidt and Pearl's System Z^+ Goldszmidt and Pearl [1996].

Definition 37 (Priority Assignment) *[Goldszmidt and Pearl, 1996, pp. 71] Given a set Δ^+ of conditionals δ_i augmented by a parameter σ_i, $\Delta^+ = \{\delta_i : \phi \xrightarrow{\sigma_i} \psi\}$, the priority assignment π is given by the Z^+-ordering on conditionals, such that $\pi(\delta_i)$ coincides with $Z^+(\delta_i)$, where is defined by Goldszmidt and Pearl [1996] as follows:*

$$Z^+(\delta_i) = min\{k^+(w) : w \vDash \phi \wedge \psi\} + \sigma(\delta_i) \tag{3.10}$$

where $k^+(w)$ is the ranking of models, defined by

$$k^+(w) = \begin{cases} \infty & \text{iff } w \not\vDash L \\ 0 & \text{iff } w \vDash L \cup D \\ 1 + \max_{\delta_m \in D_i : w \not\vDash \delta_m} Z^+(\delta_m) & \text{otherwise} \end{cases} \tag{3.11}$$

The partitioning of D under Z^+-procedure defines a mutually exclusive and exhaustive ordering among defaults based on a unique minimal rank. Given the new ordering of the set D of defaults, now a preference relation among defaults can be established.

Definition 38 *Assume that $\overline{D}_w$ represents the set of defaults falsified by an interpretation w. Then we denote by $v_i(w)$ the number of defaults belonging to partition D_i falsified by w, that is, $v_i(w) = |D_i \cap \overline{D}_w|$.*

As in Lexicographic Closure of Benferhat *et al.* or Lehmann as well, each interpretation w is associated to a tuple of $n + 1$ natural numbers $\langle v_n(w), ..., v_0(w) \rangle$. The preference relation given by the lexicographic ordering (see Definition 30) remains the same:

Definition 39 *[Lex^+-Preference] An interpretation w_p is preferred wrt an interpretation w_q, $w_p \prec w_q$, iff $\langle v_n(w_p), ..., v_0(w_p) \rangle < \langle v_n(w_q), ..., v_0(w_q) \rangle$, where $<$ is a lexicographic ordering under natural numbers.*

So, a lexicographic preference relation is established between models, and a minimal interpretation is the interpretation which there exists no interpretation that are preferred to it.

Definition 40 (Minimal Interpretation) *An interpretation w_p is a minimal interpretation with respect to lexicographic ordering iff there is no w_q such that $w_q \prec w_p$, that is, iff there is no interpretation that is preferred to w_p with respect to lexicographic ordering.*

Expressed in terms of world ranking, we say that a model w of a set of classical formulas $\mathcal{F}$ is a Lex^+-preferred model of $\mathcal{F}$ iff no model of $\mathcal{F}$ is Lex^+-preferable to w. We are now ready to define the consequence relation in Lex^+ semantics.

Definition 41 (Lex^+-Entailment) *A conditional $\delta_i : \phi_i \xrightarrow{\sigma_i} \psi_i$ is Lex^+-entailed by (Δ^+, σ_i) at strength τ, denoted by $\Delta^+ \mid\!\sim_{Lex^+} \delta_i$, iff all preferred interpretation with respect to Lex^+-ordering that satisfies ϕ_i also satisfies ψ_i.*

From now on, we say $\mid\!\sim$ and Δ instead of $\mid\!\sim_{Lex^+}$ and Δ^+, respectively, whenever it is clear from the context.

■ EXAMPLE 3.6

Given the set Δ of legal conditionals with variable strength σ of Example 3.5, a 3-tuple is assigned to each model as depicted in Figure 3.2.3. It is clear that Lex^+ also entails the conditional "the consent caused an environmental damage", that is, $w_{12} \prec w_{11}$:

$$Lex^+(c \wedge ed) = \langle 0, 0, 1 \rangle < \langle 0, 1, 1 \rangle = Lex^+(c \wedge \neg ed)$$

w_i	t	l	c	ed	Lex^+
w_1	F	F	F	F	$\langle 0,0,0 \rangle$
w_2	F	F	F	T	$\langle 0,0,0 \rangle$
w_3	F	F	T	F	$\langle 1,0,0 \rangle$
w_4	F	F	T	T	$\langle 1,0,0 \rangle$
w_5	F	T	F	F	$\langle 0,0,0 \rangle$
w_6	F	T	F	T	$\langle 0,0,0 \rangle$
w_7	F	T	T	F	$\langle 2,0,0 \rangle$
w_8	F	T	T	T	$\langle 2,0,0 \rangle$

w_i	t	l	c	ed	Lex^+
w_9	T	F	F	F	$\langle 0,1,1 \rangle$
w_{10}	T	F	F	T	$\langle 0,0,1 \rangle$
w_{11}	T	F	T	F	$\langle 0,1,1 \rangle$
w_{12}	T	F	T	T	$\langle 0,0,1 \rangle$
w_{13}	T	T	F	F	$\langle 0,1,0 \rangle$
w_{14}	T	T	F	T	$\langle 0,0,0 \rangle$
w_{15}	T	T	T	F	$\langle 1,1,0 \rangle$
w_{16}	T	T	T	T	$\langle 1,0,0 \rangle$

Figure 3.4 The Lex^+-tuples for the trespass example.

Notice that if we assign strength 4 to δ_2, $\delta_2' : t \xrightarrow{4} ed$, Lex^+ still entails such consequence:

$$Lex^+(c \wedge ed) = \langle 0,0,1 \rangle < \langle 1,0,1 \rangle = Lex^+(c \wedge \neg ed)$$

Notice that it does not matter how strong are the conditionals belonging to lower partitions. The system always will prefer to violate all these conditionals instead of violating one conditional of higher partition. Thus, the problem of accrual of reasons is not solved yet.

3.3 Modeling Legal Reasoning with Conditional Logics

In this Section, I shall introduce a model for legal reasoning having the Lex^+ Semantics as its underlying logic. We start by describing the structure of the framework, and then we shall explore whether it has a behavior that captures legal reasoning patterns.

3.3.1 Basic Framework

A legal system Δ is a tuple (L, D), where L is a set of extreme legal norms, denoted by $\phi \Rightarrow \psi$ and D is a set of defeasible legal norms, denoted by $\phi \rightarrow \psi$. The former is interpreted as "If ϕ then definitely ψ ought to be observed" whilst the latter is interpreted as "If ϕ then *prima-facie* ψ ought to be observed". Notice that $\Rightarrow$ and $\rightarrow$ are metaconnectives for legal reasoning. Each legal norm has a conditional structure, where the antecedent *describes* a fact that can possibly occur, and the consequent *prescribes* a behavior that ought to be observed. When the legal norm is unconditional, that is, when it does not have an antecedent to fire its applicability, it will be written as $\top \rightarrow \psi$. A rule or a precedent may have a conditional structure or not, but principles, goals and values are always unconditioned norms. Some facts may reach such norms in a certain degree, and a principle of a goal can be a reason for a certain outcome.

The Lexicographic Closure of Lehmann suffices to capture the inference in law based only upon the specificity relation and upon inheritance of exceptional information. Let us take the following example to demonstrate it:

🖥 EXAMPLE 3.7

Consider the following legal knowledge base:

$$\Delta = \begin{cases} \delta_1: & fe & \rightarrow & \neg w \\ \delta_2: & fe & \rightarrow & \neg lt \\ \delta_3: & d & \rightarrow & fe \\ \delta_4: & d & \rightarrow & lt \\ \delta_5: & l & \rightarrow & w \\ \delta_6: & l & \Rightarrow & d \\ \delta_7: & sl & \Rightarrow & d \end{cases} \tag{3.12}$$

Rules δ_i represent the following situations: $[\delta_1]$ one's mind expression (fe) is normally not through writing $(\neg w)$ and $[\delta_2]$ does not *prima-facie* entitle a claim for liability in tort $(\neg lt)$, $[\delta_3]$ a defamation (d) is normally one's mind expression (fe) but $[\delta_4]$ *prima-facie* entitles a claim for tort liability (lt), $[\delta_5]$ a libel (l) is normally through writing (w) and $[\delta_6]$ is definitely a defamation (d), $[\delta_7]$ a slander (sl) is definitely a defamation (d).

This set of legal information is regarded to whether the defendant is liable for damages for defamation (libel or slander) by utterances deeming the plaintiff, or the expression is insulated from tort liability, applying the constitutional privilege to speak one's mind (freedom of expression). In USA law, the precedent emphasizing the constitutional privilege of freedom of expression is *New York Times v. Sullivan*.

Based on the priority assignment on conditionals of Definition 37, the strength of each legal norm is assigned as follows:

$$Z^+(\delta_1) = Z^+(\delta_2) = 0$$
$$Z^+(\delta_3) = Z^+(\delta_4) = Z^+(\delta_5) = 1$$

Thus, the priority assignment yields the partitioning of Δ required for Lex^+ Semantics. Notice that the conditional sentences δ_6 and δ_7 are not in the partitioning, because they are strict legal norms. Recall that strict legal norms must be satisfied. A legal system that falsifies a strict legal norm is inconsistent.

We can easily see that Lex^+ entails that *a slander is not through writing* and also that *the utterances entitle the plaintiff for a claim for liability in tort against the defendant*:

$$Lex^+(sl \wedge \neg w) = \langle 0, 1 \rangle < \langle 0, 2 \rangle = Lex^+(sl \wedge w)$$

$$Lex^+(sl \wedge lt) = \langle 0, 1 \rangle < \langle 1, 0 \rangle = Lex^+(sl \wedge \neg lt)$$

Notice that in this example Lex^+ Semantics entailed the same consequences as those sanctioned by its "flat" system, that is, Lehmann's Lexicographic Closure, since all conditionals were assigned the variable strength zero.

3.3.2   Modeling Collision Meta-rules

As we have seen in Section 1.4.1 of Chapter 1, there are three collision meta-rules to solve the priority problem in law: (i) specificity; (ii) hierarchy; and (iii) temporal.

The meta-rule of specificity is naturally embedded in Lehmann's Lexicographic Closure through the partitioning of Δ given by System Z. Therefore, nothing else is needed to sanction a legal consequence respecting the specificity relations that can be found in legal norms.

To the others collision meta-rules, it is not so trivial to form a priority relation, since there exists no specificity relation between them. A possible solution is by changing the interpretation of the rule that establishes the priority relation. For instance, in example 3.1, δ_3 is the conditional that establishes the priority between δ_1 and δ_4. If we abstract the meaning of such rule, interpreting δ_3 as an hierarchy relation instead of a specificity relation, then we would conclude that δ_4 has higher hierarchy than δ_1 (i.e., c is at higher rank than t), keeping the same notation. The same assumption could be made to the temporal criterion.

However, this approach has several shortcomings, since it would yield ambiguity in the priority relation. If so, one would not know what kind of priority was established (whether specificity, hierarchy or temporality). Moreover, it does not allow reasoning about priorities, that is, defeasible priorities. In certain circumstances, we need to establish priorities between priority relations: which one should prevail? Specificity? Hierarchy? And interpreting the conditional which gives priority freely, will exclude such feature.

So, I shall claim a different solution in this work, that is, partitioning each partition D_i, in subpartitions, where we can place a legal norm according to its hierarchical level given by the *Stufenbau* (see Section 1.2.2 of Chapter 1) and then according to the temporal criterion. When there exists no exceptionality relation between two legal norms, (i) a higher level norm should prevail: Constitution over rules or precedents, rules or precedents over particular judicial decisions and so forth; or (ii) a later norm should prevail over the earlier. Thus, if we have a legal rule δ_i and a constitutional rule δ_j without any specificity relation between them (that is, in the same partition of System Z), then we should assign to each norm a different *strength* σ, which will establish the hierarchical or the temporal priority relation between δ_i and δ_j. This yields a partitioning of each partition, respecting the priority of more specific rules (undercutting) and, in the case of same partition with no specificity relation (rebutting), with priority to hierarchy.

Therefore, the priority relations of collision metarules can be established in the following:

1. Lex Specialis Derogat Generali

This collision metarule is naturally embedded in System Z^+ and it is also respected in Lex^+ System. Recall, for instance, Example 3.1. Each partition of D_i is a priority relation established over more specific information. Thus, no further extension is necessary.

■ EXAMPLE 3.8

Take the following knowledge base:

$$\Delta = \begin{cases} \delta_1 : & \phi & \rightarrow & \psi \\ \delta_2 : & \varphi & \rightarrow & \neg\psi \\ \delta_3 : & \varphi & \rightarrow & \phi \end{cases} \tag{3.13}$$

One can easily see that δ_2 is more specific than δ_1.

2. LEX SUPERIOR DEROGAT INFERIORI

In the so-called hierarchical criterion, a legal norm δ_i is admissible with respect to Δ (see Section 1.2.2 of Chapter 1), if it is enacted under authorization of another legal norm δ_j, such that the latter has priority over the former (hierarchy).

Thus, each partition D_i is also partitioned into $(S_1, S_2, ..., S_n)$, ordered according to the Kelsen's *Stufenbau*. It is assigned a parameter σ to each norm belonging to a partition S_i, such that $\sigma(\delta_m) > \sigma(\delta_n)$ iff

- $\delta_m \in D_i$ and $\delta_n \in D_i$
- $\delta_m \in S_j$ and $\delta_n \in S_k$, for all $j < k \leq n$.

■ EXAMPLE 3.9

Consider the following legal knowledge base Δ:

$$\Delta = \begin{cases} \delta_1 : & (c \wedge \phi) & \xrightarrow{\sigma_1} & \psi \\ \delta_2 : & (r \wedge \phi) & \xrightarrow{\sigma_2} & \neg\psi \\ \delta_3 : & \varphi & \longrightarrow & \neg\psi \\ \delta_4 : & \varphi & \longrightarrow & (c \wedge \phi) \end{cases} \tag{3.14}$$

where (c) stands for *constitution* and (r) for *statutory rule* (general norm according to the *Stufenbau*. Notice that there exists no specificity relation between δ_1 and δ_2, and the priority will be given by the hierarchical structure of the law, such that the Constitution has priority over legal rules. The propositions (c) and (r) were included to keep the consistency of Δ. Observe, also, that Δ respects the specificity, and if we have φ then δ_3 prevails over δ_1. Although it may look surprising a more specific lower rule overriding a more general higher rule, it does occur in legal reasoning. For instance, the constitution protects the freedom of expression. However, a lower-level rule prohibits the defamation, which is a kind of expression. Although having been a kind of one's mind expression, a lower-level rule prohibiting defamation is more specific than the higher-level norm and thus should prevail.

3. SPECIAL CASE: DEFEASIBILITY OF PRIORITIES

There may occur a clash between specificity and hierarchy principles. As we have seen in Section 1.4.1 of Chapter 1, both are strong criteria, and there is no further criterion to solve this collision. The rule of thumb of commonsense reasoning prefers to favour the specificity over all other criteria. Hence, the specificity relation should have priority over hierarchy. Whereas the hierarchy relation is kept at the legal validity level (authoritative issuance), we may preserve the priority on specificity (a lower norm that establishes a non-admissible exception should not belong to Δ). But, the validity definition does not say anything about the content of the norm and we cannot make such assumption. Recall that it is impossible to know the contents of a lower norm only by looking at the content of a higher norm (see Section 1.2.2 of Chapter 1). So, a lower norm can be more specific than a higher norm. Thus, there are strong reasons to keep the specificity criterion as the most powerful one.

Nevertheless, there may occur a situation when we must abandon the priority based on the specificity relation in favor of the hierarchy relation. There may come a point when it seems more reasonable from a legal point of view to abandon accepting the more specific rule in favor of accepting a higher one. This is the case when a more specific rule excludes essential properties of higher rules. Thus, it may be more reasonable to reject the belief in an exceptional norm, when it displays no such attributes, rather than insisting on it; it may be more reasonable rejecting a more specific legal rule claiming that it violates a higher norm (viz., the Constitution) rather than excluding the higher one. If we think upon the penguin example, it may be more reasonable rejecting that a penguin is a bird, when it exhibits none of bird attributes such as the ability to fly, wings, feathers, beaks, rather than insisting that it is an exceptional bird.

In another example, when we have a clash between the information given by a recognized scientist and information given by a child, there is not specificity relation (since a scientist is not a child), but we may trust more on the information given by the former rather than those given by the latter. If this is the case, then we should abandon the ε-consistency of a legal knowledge base Δ (which is based on specificity), assigning freely the priority over a legal norm δ_i, such that the specificity is no longer observed. This is also possible in the present formalism, requiring only the extension of Lex^+ semantics to Benferhat's et al Lexicographical Ordering (viz. Benferhat *et al.* [1993]).

Hence, in the case that an exceptional clause excludes an essential property of a higher norm, the strength of a conditional is freely assigned by the user. Then, $\sigma(\delta_m) > \sigma(\delta_n)$ if

- $\delta_m \in S_j$ and $\delta_n \in S_k$, for all $j < k \leq n$
- $\delta_m \in D_i$ and $\delta_n \in D_{i+1}$

In other words, although belonging to a higher partition of D_i (more specific), δ_n is outweighed by δ_m, which have a higher hierarchy. Notice that identifying these situations in legal philosophy still remains as an open problem. Sometimes it is accepted that a lower-level norm creates an exception to the constitution. However, in certain situations, the exception created is not accepted from the legal point of view, and the lower-level norm is considered unconstitutional (lack of social validity of the lower-level norm, since there should be no compliance with the norm and no sanction for non-compliance).

▣ EXAMPLE 3.10

In Example 3.9, the conditional δ_3 has priority over δ_1, since the former is more specific than the latter. However, if δ_1 exhibits an essential property of a higher norm, than it should have priority over δ_3. In this case, the variable strength of δ_1 should be greater than the rank κ^+ of δ_3, that is, $\sigma(\delta_1) > \kappa^+(\delta_2)$.

4. LEX POSTERIOR DEROGAT PRIORI

The assumptions required to formalize *Lex Posterior* collision metarule are the same to the *Lex Superior* one. The only difference is the following. The temporal metarule is a weak criterion, whilst the others two are strong criteria. Hence, the temporal metarule must respect the others collision rules.

Each partition S_i is also partitioned into $(T_1, ..., T_n)$, ordered according to time sequence. It is assigned a parameter σ to each $\delta_m \in T_i$, such that $\sigma(\delta_m) > \sigma(\delta_n)$ iff

- $\delta_m \in D_i$ and $\delta_n \in D_i$
- $\delta_m \in S_i$ and $\delta_n \in S_i$
- $\delta_m \in T_j$ and $\delta_n \in T_i$, for all $j > i$.

Let us see the collision meta-rules in the running example.

▣ EXAMPLE 3.11   Collision Meta-rules

Assume that the legal knowledge base Δ given in example 3.7 is augmented with the following norms:

$$\Delta' = \Delta \cup \begin{cases} \delta_8 : & r \wedge utv \xrightarrow{\ 2\ } l \\ \delta_9 : & p \wedge utv \xrightarrow{\ 1\ } \neg l \end{cases} \tag{3.15}$$

where (r) stands for *rule*, (p) for *precedent* (judicial decision) and (utv) meaning *utterances appeared on television*. There have been judicial decisions (precedents) regarding defamation by television as having been not a libel (δ_9), whilst the Restatement (Second) of Torts § 568 A (USA law) characterize it as libel (δ_8). According to the hierarchy principle of civil law systems, the statute overrules the precedent (case reversed by statute in common law systems). Notice that there exists no specificity relation among δ_8 and δ_9.

Since δ_8 and δ_9 are tolerated by each other, Z^+ of each norm is equal to the strength σ_i that is assigned to each one. So, $Z^+(\delta_8) = 2$ and $Z^+(\delta_9) = 1$. On an interpretation with r, p and utv, we have the following consequence relation under Lex^+ semantics:

$$Lex^+(p, r, utv, l) = \langle 0, 1 \rangle < \langle 1, 0 \rangle = Lex^+(p, r, utv, \neg l)$$

Therefore, Lex^+ can sanction a consequence respecting the specificity and the hierarchy between legal norms.

However, it is not always that collision rules solve the problem of priority of norms in legal reasoning. It is very common, rather, that neither a collision rule is given nor is it sufficient to give a right answer to the problems that arise from collision of legal norms having no specificity, hierarchy of temporal relation between them.

Moreover, even when the plaintiff or the defendant can argue a collision metarule to solve the priority problem, such metarules are also defeasible and subject to exception by stronger reasons. After all, Collision Mera-rules are just reasons. Reasons for or reasons against a particular legal outcome. Therefore, even collision meta-rules can be weighed against other reasons, likewise when we have two strong criteria such as specificity and hierarchy, or when we have an ordinary rule with an exception to the meta-rule. If this is the case, the priority should be reached by weighing and balancing all relevant reasons. But this is not the only the justification why we need a weighing process. Actually, there exist several norms that have to be weighed against each other, since they show none specificity, such as principles, values, goals or indirect evidence for a conclusion. This feature will be formalized in the next Section.

3.3.3 Weighing and Balancing

Recall that weighing and balancing (Section 1.4.2 of Chapter 1) is a process where a set of reasons for an outcome and a set of reasons against that outcome are placed on the scale of a balance, and the "heavier" set (that is, the most acceptable) outweighs the other one. As long as the weighing process is based in such incompatible sets of reasons, and since it should consider as many reasons as possible, it should be included in Δ all relevant circumstances that we expect to be weighed and that are actually known.

3.3.3.1 *Setting the Relevant Circumstances*   Relevant circumstances are reasons. Such reasons can be generated by a principle, a goal and so forth. Now, we should be able to determine logically whether these reasons are relevant or not for a certain weighing process. A normative proposition supports or is a *relevant circumstance* for a conclusion if and only if the normative proposition strengthens the belief (or the disbelief) in an outcome. Or, saying in 'weighing metaphor' language, if and only if the proposition enhances the weight or the outweigh of the conclusion. Thus, if the weight of a conclusion, given a certain reason, is greater than the weight of such outcome *without* that reason, than such is a relevant circumstance for weighing.

Note that this definition specially holds in Ranking Functions Spohn [1994]. Given a ranking function κ and a normative argument $\phi \rightarrow \psi$, we can say that φ is a relevant circumstance for ψ if and only if the belief in ψ given φ is stronger than given $\neg\varphi$.

Since a circumstance can either be irrelevant or strengthens a belief in an upper or lower level, such can be an irrelevant reason, a positive reason or a negative reason, respectively. A principle or a goal, for instance, expressed in the proposition φ is a (positive) reason for ψ given ϕ if and only if the rank κ of the conditional "φ and ϕ entails ψ" has a greater degree than the rank κ of the conditional "non-φ and ϕ entails ψ". Formally:

Definition 42 *Spohn [1994] A normative proposition φ is a (positive) reason for ψ given ϕ iff*

$$\kappa(\varphi \wedge \phi \rightarrow \psi) > \kappa(\neg\varphi \wedge \phi \rightarrow \psi)$$

If the rank *kappa* of the former conditional is smaller than the rank of the latter conditional, then φ is a (negative) reason for ψ given ϕ:

Definition 43 *Spohn [1994] A normative proposition φ is a (negative) reason for ψ given ϕ iff*

$$\kappa(\varphi \wedge \phi \rightarrow \psi) < \kappa(\neg\varphi \wedge \phi \rightarrow \psi)$$

Finally, if the rank *kappa* of both conditionals is equal, then the reason is irrelevant for weighing and balancing:

Definition 44 *Spohn [1994] A normative proposition φ is an (irrelevant) reason for ψ given ϕ iff*

$$\kappa(\varphi \wedge \phi \rightarrow \psi) = \kappa(\neg\varphi \wedge \phi \rightarrow \psi)$$

Based on these definitions, one should consider as many relevant reasons as possible (or at least as many relevant reasons as it is allowed by procedural rules) in weighing and balancing. However, the relevant circumstances can behave differently, if they are dependent or independent of another relevant reason. Such feature will be discussed in the next section.

3.3.3.2 *Accrual of Reasons* Although a reason is considered relevant for weighing, it may happen that such cannot have strength enough to endow an outcome, as we have seen in Section 1.4.2 of Chapter 1. To deal with indirect evidence, Goldszmidt and Pearl Goldszmidt and Pearl [1996] distinguish between two different evidential reports, by invoking specialized conditioning operators, unconstrained by the semantics of rules. They remark that although one may think that variable strength conditionals embedded in System Z^+ would automatically provide such a method, there are some shortcomings to this approach. The first one is due to the convenience of treating *if-then* rules as a stable part of our knowledge, and as such unperturbed by any particular set of observations. The second one is based on the assumption that evidence should accumulate, whilst rules do not, that is, evidence is conditionally independent. Hence, they proposed a method distinguishing Type-J ("all-things-considered") and Type-L ("Nothing-else-considered") to incorporate the cumulative pooling of evidence.

This assumption is also convenient in weighing and balancing. At first glance it might seem that weighing should be based only on *all-things-considered* normative arguments (cf. Peczenik [1989]), even whether we emphasize the *ceteris paribus* all-things-considered statements. However, as far as I see, weighing and balancing also calls for a more restrictive set of relevant circumstances than the *ceteris paribus* all-things-considered statements. In legal reasoning, sometimes the piece of information is not precise enough to be a stable part of our knowledge, and the circumstances - be they an evidence, a legal principle or a goal - provide merely indirect reasons in favor of the conclusion. In this case, the two or more reasons together should endow a conclusion that is stronger than any one observation in isolation would do. This suggests the existence of a set of (independent) reasons in law just as described by Goldszmidt and Pearl. Likewise, such will be referred to in this essay as *nothing-else-considered* arguments.

When we have only indirect or soft reasons for an outcome (as in weighing and balancing), the parameter that increases the *'degree of strength'* of such conditional should not shift the current belief of the proposition to a new level (rank), but rather to a new degree only. This will permit us to provide two independent reasons for an outcome, such that the two reasons together endow the outcome with a strength that is stronger than any one reason in isolation.

With Lex^+ system, it seems to be possible to derive a conclusion after weighing and balancing a set of reasons for and a set of reasons against a state of affairs, even when those are merely indirect of soft reasons. If one considers all relevant circumstances, and if the reasons are a stable part of our knowledge ("hard" reasons), then the conclusion is undisturbed by any other set of relevant circumstances. One can think on it as an all-things-considered outcome, and the current belief in the conclusion should be in a specific level. However, if one considers some relevant circumstances, and the reasons are merely indirect ("soft" reasons), then the reasons should accumulate. In this case, one may have a nothing-else-considered outcome, and the separate degree of belief to each reason should be shifted by some degree, although it is not shifted to a new level of belief.

Thus, if one considers as many reasons as possible to the task of weighing, one can yield *ceteris paribus* all-things-considered (if κ is on a specific level) or the variant nothing-else-considered obligation (if κ is augmented in some degree only).

Up to this point, some features of weighing were naturally embedded, like the clash of arguments (negative and positive reasons) and the inheritance of arguments with no relevance to the decision (irrelevant reasons). The last feature is the so-called *accrual of reasons* which can be embodied in Lex^+ Semantics as well. For such account, we should revise the rank of a proposition according to the strength on a belief.

3.3.3.3 *Ceteris Paribus All-Things-Considered Obligations*   According to Goldszmidt and Pearl [1996], in all-things-considered obligations, the conditional degree of belief normally is not changed by an observation reported of on the evidence ϕ or on the evidence $\neg\phi$. So, letting κ and κ' denote the ranking before and after the observation respectively, we have:

$$\kappa'(\psi) = \min[\kappa(\psi|\phi) + \kappa'(\phi); \kappa(\psi|\neg\phi) + \kappa'(\neg\phi)] \tag{3.16}$$

where $\kappa'(\phi) = 0$ and $\kappa'(\neg\phi) = \sigma$, and σ denotes the strength of the observation. Notice that this process is equivalent to ordinary Bayesian conditioning, if $\kappa(\neg\phi) = \infty$. However, this ranking is not commutative yet. Moreover, if ϕ_1 and ϕ_2 are dependent propositions[3], the order in which $\kappa(\neg\phi_1) = \sigma_1$ and $\kappa(\neg\phi_2) = \sigma_2$ are established might yield different results. This behaviour is expected in the *all-things-considered* approach, since the last report summarizes *all* previous observations.

3.3.3.4 *Nothing-Else-Considered Obligations*   In a *nothing-else-considered* interpretation Goldszmidt and Pearl [1996], some indirect reasons should accumulate such that a new evidence or a principle would support a proposition ϕ to degree σ, shifting the belief of ϕ to some degree but not to the absolute value of the final belief in ϕ.

$$\kappa'(\phi) - \kappa'(\neg\phi) = \kappa(\phi) - \kappa(\neg\phi) - \sigma \tag{3.17}$$

and, since either $\kappa'(\phi)$ or $\kappa'(\neg\phi)$ must be zero, we obtain

$$\kappa'(\phi) = \max[0; \kappa(\phi) - \kappa(\neg\phi) - \sigma] \tag{3.18}$$

$$\kappa'(\neg\phi) = \max[0; \kappa(\neg\phi) - \kappa(\phi) + \sigma] \tag{3.19}$$

This conditioning shifts the difference between the ranks $\kappa(\phi)$ and $\kappa(\neg\phi)$ by the assigned strength σ. Then, the resulting $\kappa'(\phi)$ is used to compute the $\kappa'(\psi)$ for an arbitrary wff ψ:

---

[3]We say that ϕ_1 and ϕ_2 are dependent iff $\kappa(\phi_2|\phi_1) \neq \kappa(\phi_2)$.

$$\kappa'(\psi) = \begin{cases} \min[\kappa(\psi|\phi) + \kappa(\phi) - \kappa(\neg\phi) - \sigma; \kappa(\psi|\neg\phi)] & \text{if } \kappa(\neg\phi) + \kappa(\phi) < \sigma \\ \min[\kappa(\psi|\phi); \kappa(\psi|\neg\phi) + \kappa(\neg\phi) + \sigma - \kappa(\phi)] & \text{if } \kappa(\neg\phi) + \kappa(\phi) > \sigma \\ \min[\kappa(\psi|\phi); \kappa(\psi|\neg\phi)] & \text{if } \kappa(\neg\phi) + \kappa(\phi) = \sigma \end{cases}$$

$$(3.20)$$

This ranking is commutative and hence it respects evidence independence. Therefore, the rank of ϕ (relative to $\neg\phi$) is shifted by the strengths σ_1 and σ_2 of two soft reasons (evidence or principles), that is, by $\sigma_1 + \sigma_2$, as is expected in the accrual of reasons.

Once we have the revised rank κ' of an outcome from indirect evidence, it is included in the partitioned Δ. So, D_i is thus Z^+ ordered, though shifted adequately by the relative strength of indirect evidence, yielding the partitioning of D_i required by Lex^+ Semantics.

Nevertheless, this approach still has a gap, that is, the attribution of the strength of each indirect reason which should be weighed. In Goldszmidt and Pearl method, it is left up to the user for finding and assigning the specific value of each evidence. However, there exists an attractive method proposed for balancing legal principles, that can supply the strength. Such will be discussed in the next section.

3.3.4 Alexy's Weight Formula

Robert Alexy, a German Professor of Law at Kiel University, introduced a method for balancing legal principles Alexy [2003], proposing a double triadic model in order to assign the arithmetical and geometrical values to each element of the weighing formula. The triadic scale is characterized by three basic stages represented by the letters "l", "m" and "s", standing respectively for *light*(minor, weak), *moderate* and *serious* (high, strong). A simple and highly instructive method for allocating numbers to these three stages is either taking a geometric sequence 2^0, 2^1 and 2^2, or an arithmetic sequence 1, 2 and 3:

triadic scale	geometrical	arithmetical
l	$2^0 = 1$	1
m	$2^1 = 2$	2
s	$2^2 = 4$	3

Then, Alexy extends the triadic model to a double-triadic model by applying the three classes in turn to each other, yielding a nine-stage model:

double-triadic	geometrical	arithmetical
ll	$2^0 = 1$	1
lm	$2^1 = 2$	2
ls	$2^2 = 4$	3
ml	$2^3 = 8$	4
mm	$2^4 = 16$	5
ms	$2^5 = 32$	6
sl	$2^6 = 64$	7
sm	$2^7 = 128$	8
ss	$2^8 = 256$	9

where the letters express the following: very trivial (*ll*) and minor interferences in the middle (*lm*) or in the upper range (*ls*), moderate interferences at the bottom (*ml*), in the middle (*mm*) or at the top of the range (*ms*), and less serious (*sl*), moderately serious (*sm*) and very serious (*ss*) interferences.

The double-triadic method is the limit of the refinement of the scale to be understandable. Alexy writes:

> It is of considerable interest that the descriptions of these nine classes are quite easy to understand, whereas already the classes of a threefold-triadic model would become, apart from the areas at the extremes, incomprehensible. How, for example, is one supposed to understand "seriously slightly moderate"? It seems that this conjunction of three classes exceeds our power of understanding; if not, a conjunction of four classes would surely do.

To calculate the concrete weight of a legal principle, Alexy proposed the following "weight formula" for the geometrical sequence:

$$W_{i,j} = \frac{I_i \cdot W_i \cdot R_i}{I_j \cdot W_j \cdot R_j} \tag{3.21}$$

where ($W_{i,j}$) represents the final weight of the principle (i) that conflicts with principle (j). (I) stands for the concrete impact of the interference on both principles, (W) represents the abstract weight of each principle and (R) stands for the reliability of the empirical assumptions concerning what the measure in question means for the non-realization of such principles.

A formula for the arithmetical sequence is also possible:

$$W_{i,j} = I_i + W_i + R_i - I_j - W_j - R_j \tag{3.22}$$

Actually, Alexy speaks in his paper only about $W_{i,j} = I_i - I_j$. Also, Alexy claims that the arithmetical sequence will not be as instructive as the geometrical sequences, if the triadic model is extended to a double-triadic scale.

A word upon the variables. The variable I_i is always concrete (depending on the circumstances of the concrete case) and represents the degree of *interference* ("degree of non-satisfaction or detriment"), that is, the effects which the omission of the interference with the principle P_i would have for P_j. The variable W_i is always abstract (i.e., it is independent of the circumstances of any cases). Some constitutional principles do not differ in their abstract weight while others do. If they do not differ, the abstract weigh can be disregard in balancing. The last variable, R_i, is epistemic and concerns to the reliability of the empirical assumptions of the circumstances of the concrete case. This reflects the distinction of the *BundesVerfassungsGerichte* (German Federal Constitutional Court) upon the intensity of the review (BVerfGE vol. 50, 290, 333 *apud* Alexy [2003]): "intensive review" (certain or reliable), "plausibility review" (maintainable or plausible) and "evidential review" (not evidently false).

Governing variables I_i and R_i, Alexy proposes respectively the first (substantive) and the second (epistemic) Law of Balancing:

Definition 45 (Substantive Law of Balancing) *Alexy [2003] The greater the degree of non-satisfaction of, or detriment to, one right or principle, the greater must be the importance of satisfying the other.*

Definition 46 (Epistemic Law of Balancing) *Alexy [2003] The more heavily an interference with a constitutional right weighs, the greater must be the certainty of its underlying premisses.*

Alexy's "weight formula" is attractive and clear, supplying an elegant method to measure principles in collision. However, it has some limitations, for instance, the number of colliding principles, the lack of clarity of the weight of the circumstances, etc.

I propose in this work a different method based on the qualitative probability given by System Lex^+ and on the two evidential reports given by Goldszmidt and Pearl [1996]. The introduced method presented better results in all tests performed with the two approaches.

In an attempt to reconcile the two methods, I used the double-triadic method of Alexy's formula to establish the individual strength of each variable strength conditional. Therefore, the strength σ on an observation that supports ϕ shall be given by the arithmetical sequence of Alexy's double-triadic method.

But that's not the only method I used on this research. A more complete result was yielded with the use of the System introduced in this research to calculate the variable strength applied to each conditional. That is, the strength σ is calculated using the very System Lex^+ on itself - obviously, with different arguments. In other words, the strength σ is calculated recursively by applying Lex^+ to the circumstances for and against the conditional strengthens by σ

The full comparison of the results of both theories remains to be investigated.

3.3.5   Legal, Social and Ethical Validity through Lex^+ Semantics

In Section 1.2.2 of Chapter 1 we have seen that the validity of a lower-level norm depends on the accordance of its contents to the frame of a higher-level norm. This observation justified the requirement of consistency of Δ whenever a norm δ_i is added to Δ. However, the notion of consistency in classical logics cannot handle conflicting information, and thus, it is not possible to build a consistent Δ with conflicting norms. Recall that in classical logics the axiom of monotonicity refrains the addition of more specific information to Δ. We need, thus, an admissibility notion that allows a non-monotonic behavior, though preserving other important properties of classical logic. So, we must revise the definition of admissible legal norms in the following:

Definition 47 (Authoritative Issuance Revisited) *A legal norm* $\delta_i : \phi_i \xrightarrow{\sigma_i} \psi_i$ *is authoritatively issued iff*

1. δ_i *is a member of rational closure of* Δ.

2. δ_i *is issued by an organ authorized by* $\delta_j \in \Delta$, *for some* $\delta_j \prec \delta_i$.

3. δ_i *is issued following the process established by* $\delta_j \in \Delta$, *for some* $\delta_j \prec \delta_i$.

Since the admissibility of norms on Δ is based also in issuance, the definition of admissible legal norms requires now the consistency under rational inference relations (see Section 2.2.1 of Chapter 2), preserving some important properties of the provability operator $\vdash$. The definition of valid norms given by 6 remains the same, though now it refers to a different class of legal norms. Thus, Δ may have now inconsistent information, as a legal rule in which killing is prohibited and another rule in which killing in self defence is permitted.

Nevertheless, we also need to translate the correctness definition given in 8 to the terms of ranking functions. Recall that the acceptance of an argument δ_i requires that the argument δ_j against δ_i is outweighed by Δ. Expressed in terms of ranking functions, also including variable strength defaults, the definition 7 is revised as follows:

Definition 48 (Acceptable Legal Norm Revisited) *A legal norm* $\delta_i : \phi \xrightarrow{\sigma} \psi$ *is acceptable with respect to a normative system* Δ *iff* $\kappa(\phi_i \wedge \psi_i) + \sigma_i < \kappa(\phi_i \wedge \neg\psi_i)$. *That is, iff there exists no argument* $\delta_j \in \Delta$ *that outweighs* δ_i.

Notice that this definition is the same of definition 7, just expressed in terms of ranking functions with variable strength defaults. The definition 8 remains the same, and δ_i is content-correct iff it is acceptable.

Now, some important results of this research can be established.

Theorem 3.1 *A legal norm* δ_i *is legally and socially valid law wrt* Δ *iff* $\Delta \cup \{\delta_i\}$ *is* Lex^+*-consistent.*

Proof: To prove this theorem we should prove that δ_i is a member of the rational closure of Δ iff $\Delta \cup \{\delta_i\}$ is Lex^+-consistent. The others two conditions of legal validity (issuance) are exogenous conditions which cannot be logically proved, but only verified upon the addition of δ_i to Δ. Notice also that Lex^+-consistency coincides with Z^+-ordering which was proved satisfying the rational closure by yielding a rank with exclusive and exhaustive ordering among defaults (see Goldszmidt and Pearl [1996]). Hence, we have to prove that δ_i is ranked in a modular ordering according to Lex^+ Semantics (Z^+-ordering) on the set of defaults it violates. The following proof is from Lehmann [1995] which also holds for variable strength defaults since they are ordered according to Z^+-ordering.

If Part Assume that the rank of $\delta_i : \phi \xrightarrow{\sigma} \psi$ is strictly less than that of $\delta_j : \phi \to \neg\psi$, and that w is a propositional model that satisfies $\phi \wedge \psi$ and is minimal among those for the Lex^+-ordering. If δ_i has rank κ, there is a model that satisfies δ_i and violates no default of D of rank greater or equal to κ. Therefore, w violates no such default and thus satisfies no formula of rank strictly greater than κ. The model w does not satisfy $\phi \wedge \neg\psi$ and hence satisfies $\phi \wedge \psi$.

Only If Part Suppose now, that all propositional models that satisfy ϕ are minimal in the Lex^+-ordering for that property, also satisfy ψ. Let the rank of ϕ be κ. Since there is a propositional model that satisfies ϕ and violates no default of rank greater or equal to κ, all models that satisfy ϕ and violate no default of rank greater or equal to κ also satisfy ψ. Therefore, the rank of $\phi \wedge \neg\psi$ is greater than κ. ∎

Theorem 3.2 *A legal norm δ_i raises a claim to correctness with respect to a normative system Δ iff δ_i is Lex^+-entailed by Δ.*

Proof: **If Part** Assume that $\delta_i : \phi \xrightarrow{\sigma} \psi$ raises a claim to correctness with respect to Δ. Then, there exists no $\delta_j : \phi \xrightarrow{\sigma} \neg\psi$ such that the rank of δ_j is strictly lower than the rank of δ_i. To prove the if part, we should prove that δ_i is Lex^+ entailed by a conditional knowledge base Δ. By contradiction, assume that δ_i is not Lex^+ entailed by Δ, then the interpretation w_q that satisfies ϕ and ψ is not preferred, that is, there exists an interpretation w_p such that $w_p \prec w_q$, where $w_p = \phi \wedge \neg\psi$ and $w_q = \phi \wedge \psi$. According to definition 39, $w_p \prec w_q$ iff $\langle v_n(w_p), ..., v_0(w_p)\rangle < \langle v_n(w_q), ..., v_0(w_q)\rangle$, that is, the number of defaults falsified by w_p in a given index is lower than the number of defaults falsified by w_q at the same index. Hence, there exists an index u such that $v_u(w_p) < v_u(w_q)$, and for all index m belonging to the interval $u < m \le n$, we have $v_m(w_p) = v_m(w_q)$. Since the number of defaults falsified by w_p at a partition of index u is lower than the number of defaults falsified by w_q at a partition of the same index, $v_u(w_p) < v_u(w_q)$, then there exists a δ_j such that the rank of δ_j is lower than the rank of δ_i. Therefore, δ_i is not correctness. Contradiction.

Only If Part Assume that $\delta_i : \phi \xrightarrow{\sigma} \psi$ is Lex^+ entailed by a conditional knowledge base Δ and w_q is a minimal interpretation with respect to the Lex^+ ordering. Then there exists no interpretation w_p such that $w_p \prec w_q$. To prove the only if part we should prove that δ_i is correctness with respect to Δ, that is, there is no $\delta_j : \phi \longrightarrow \neg\psi$ such that the rank of δ_j is lower than the rank of δ_i. By contradiction, assume that δ_i is not correctness. Then, there exists a δ_j with a rank lower than δ_i, $\kappa(\phi \wedge \neg\psi) < \sigma + \kappa(\phi \wedge \psi)$. Since δ_j has an interpretation $w_p = \phi \wedge \neg\psi$ which has rank lower than the interpretation $w_q = \phi \wedge \psi$ of δ_i, the number of defaults falsified by w_p in an index u is lower than the number of defaults falsified by w_q at the same index u, that is, $v_u(w_p) < v_u(w_q)$, and $v_m(w_p) = v_m(w_q)$, for some $u < m \le n$. According to definition 39, w_p is preferred to w_q, $w_p \prec w_q$, iff $\langle v_n(w_p), ..., v_0(w_p) \rangle < \langle v_n(w_q), ..., v_0(w_q) \rangle$. Therefore, w_q is not a minimal interpretation with respect to the Lex^+ semantics and δ_i is not Lex^+ entailed by Δ. Contradiction. ∎

Consequently, we have a legal system Δ which is *sound* and *complete*, since if $\Delta \vdash \delta_i$ then $\Delta \vDash \delta_i$, and also if $\Delta \vDash \delta_i$ then $\Delta \vdash \delta_i$. It follows from theorem 3.2 that Lex^+ entailment does not sanction all binding norm. So, the following consequences are obtained.

Corollary 49 *All legally valid norm δ_i are binding.*

Proof: Trivial. If $\delta_i \in \Delta$, naturally δ_i will be used in the justification of an outcome, that is, $\Delta \mathbin{|\!\sim} \psi$. ∎

Corollary 50 *Not all legally valid norm δ_i raises a claim to correctness.*

Proof: The proof is immediate. Since Δ is ranked according to Z^+-ordering, then there exists a norm $\delta_i \in \Delta$ such that δ_i yields an interpretation w_p that is not minimal with respect to Lex^+ entailment, that is, there may exist an interpretation w_q such that $w_q \prec w_p$. ∎

The next Chapter proposes a translation of the Lex^+ Semantics to a Maximum Satisfiability problem.

CHAPTER 4

A MATHEMATICAL FRAMEWORK FOR CONDITIONAL LOGIC

'Αγεωμετρητος μηδεις εισιτω
(*Do not enter those who ignore geometry!*)
Advertisement in the entrance of Plato's Academy
— Elias, *Commentaria in Aristetelem Graeca* (18,118,18)

4.1 Introduction

So far now, we have a logical model for capturing the reasoning patterns in law which was proven sound and complete. In this chapter I shall describe a mathematical translation of the conditional logic used to model legal reasoning (Lex^+ System). The main idea is to capture the entailment of legal consequences through a model of 0-1 programming. For such task, we translated the Lex^+-semantics to an instance of weighted MAX-SAT problem, in order to compute the logical consequences found in legal reasoning. Hence, combinatorial optimization algorithms can be used to yield the legal consequences of defeasible reasoning over legal conditional knowledge bases.

Using mathematical programming techniques to prove theorems in classical propositional logic is not new. Actually, its roots go back to Boole's seminal work (see Hailperin [1976] and Chandru and Hooker [1999]). This approach was revived and improved by Jeroslow [1988], and later by several researchers, e.g., Hooker [1988], Bell *et al.* [1996]. In this dissertation I shall extend this approach to compute legal reasoning through a model-theoretic semantics, notably the introduced Lex^+ semantics.

4.2   The Maximum Satisfiability Problem

The satisfiability problem (SAT) is a propositional logic problem, and its goal is to determine an assignment of truth values to propositional letters that makes a given CNF satisfied or show that none exists; in other words, the goal of SAT is to find a true assignment that satisfies a given conjunctive normal form $\phi = c_1 \wedge c_2 \wedge \ldots \wedge c_n$, where each c_i is a clause.

The SAT problem is in the core of a wide class of NP-complete problems Cook [1971]. The *MAX-SAT problem* is closely related to the SAT problem, and informally is defined as: Given a collection of clauses, we seek a true assignment that minimizes the number of falsified clauses. The *weighted* MAX-SAT problem is an instance of MAX-SAT that assigns a weight to each clause and seeks a true assignment that maximizes the sum of weights of the satisfied clauses. Both problems (MAX-SAT and weighted MAX-SAT) are NP-hard problems. For a survey regarding MAX-SAT problems and their algorithms, see Gu *et al.* [1997].

Some existing connections among classical propositional logic and integer programming were shown by Williams [1976] and Jeroslow [1988]. We shall briefly summarize one of the possible translations of a CNF into a set of linear constraints, as a way to use integer programming techniques.

A literal is a propositional letter a_i or the negation of a propositional letter $\neg a_i$. A clause is a disjunction of literals. A clause is *satisfied* by an interpretation iff at least one of the literals present in the clause has "true" value. A formula ϕ of the propositional language L is said to be in "conjunctive normal form" (CNF) if ϕ is the conjunction of clauses. Each formula ϕ has equivalent CNF formulas[1]. The function $CNF(\alpha)$ returns a CNF formula that is equivalent to α. Although a formula α may have several equivalent CNF formulas, we assume that the function $CNF(.)$ maps α to only one CNF formula. A formula ϕ in CNF is said to be *satisfied* for an interpretation I iff all clauses in ϕ are satisfied. H_ϕ represents a Herbrand base of formula CNF ϕ, i.e., the set of all ground literals on formula ϕ.

Definition 51 (Binary Variables) *x is a binary variable if it can only have the integer values $\{0, 1\}$. Each binary variable is labeled with the literal with which it is related.*

---

[1] Two formulas α and β are equivalent iff $\alpha \vDash \beta$ and $\beta \vDash \alpha$.

Definition 52 (Binary Representation of a Formula) *H_ϕ is the Herbrand base associated to the formula ϕ. $B(H_\phi)$ represents the set of binary variables associated to ϕ and is formed by $P(H_\phi) \cup N(H_\phi)$, such that for each $a_i \in H_\phi$ if a_i is a positive literal then x_{a_i} belongs to $P(H_\phi)$, otherwise if a_i is a negative literal then x_{a_i} belongs to $N(H_\phi)$.*

Definition 53 (Binary Attribution) *The binary representation of H_ϕ is $B(H_\phi) = \{x_{a_1}, \ldots, x_{a_m}\}$. An attribution of binary variables is a mapping s : $B(H_\phi) \to \{0,1\}^m$.*

A binary variable x_a represents the truth value of a.

Note that throughout this work we assume that the language is finite; for this reason, we can assume that the attribution of binary variables is defined wrt any formula ϕ, i.e., wrt the binary representation of a formula ϕ.

Definition 54 (Linear Inequality) *Assume that c_i is a clause, in a propositional language L, and that $B(H_{c_i}) = P(H_{c_i}) \cup N(H_{c_i})$ represents the set of binary variables associated to c_i (definition 52). $\lambda(c_i)$ is the linear inequality generated from $B(H_{c_i})$, and it is defined as:*

$$\sum_{x_{a_k} \in P(H_{c_i})} x_{a_k} - \sum_{x_{a_k} \in N(H_{c_i})} x_{a_k} \geq 1 - |N(H_{c_i})| \qquad (4.1)$$

We can extend the definition of linear inequality generated from a clause to a system of inequalities generated from a conjunctive normal formula ϕ.

Definition 55 *ϕ is a CNF, C_ϕ is the set of clauses in ϕ; then the system of linear inequalities generated by ϕ, $sd(\phi)$, is:*

$$sd(\phi) = \{\lambda(c_i) : \text{for all } c_i \in C_\phi\} \qquad (4.2)$$

■ EXAMPLE 4.1

Consider the following conjunctive normal formula:

$$\phi = \underbrace{(a \vee b)}_{c_1} \wedge \underbrace{(\neg a \vee c \vee b)}_{c_2} \qquad (4.3)$$

The set of clauses in ϕ is $C_\phi = \{c_1, c_2\}$. The Herbrand bases of the clauses c_1 and c_2 are, respectively, $\{a, b\}$ and $\{\neg a, c, b\}$. Thus $B(H_{c_1}) = \{x_a, x_b\}$ and $B(H_{c_2}) = N(H_{c_2}) \cup P(H_{c_2})$, such that $N(H_{c_2}) = \{x_a\}$ and $P(H_{c_2}) = \{x_c, x_b\}$. Therefore, the inequality system generated by ϕ, $sd(\phi)$, is:

$$\left\{ \begin{array}{llll} \lambda(c_1): & x_a + x_b & \geq & 1 \\ \lambda(c_2): & x_c + x_b - x_a & \geq & 0 \end{array} \right\}$$

Definition 56 *A binary attribution s* satisfies *an inequality system $sd(\phi)$ iff s does not falsify any constraint in $sd(\phi)$.*

As we said before the propositional satisfiability problem for a CNF ϕ consists in finding an attribution of truth values to literals that are in ϕ which satisfies each clause in ϕ or showing that this attribution does not exist. Therefore, the propositional satisfiability problem consists on finding a binary attribution that satisfies the inequality set $sd(\phi)$, in other words, has as objective finding a solution for $sd(\phi)$ Chandru and Hooker [1999].

The MAX-SAT problem, for its turn, consists of finding an attribution of truth values to literals in ϕ that falsifies the smaller set of inequalities $\lambda(c_i)$. The weighted MAX-SAT problem assigns a weight to each inequality $\lambda(c_i)$, i.e., a weight to each clause, and seeks an assignment that minimizes the sum of the weight of falsified clauses. So, to formulate the weighted MAX-SAT problem as an integer program we first define that $\lambda(c_i)$ is equal to the following inequality:

$$\sum_{x_{a_k} \in P(H_{c_i})} x_{a_k} - \sum_{x_{a_k} \in N(H_{c_i})} x_{a_k} + t_i \geq 1 - |N(H_{c_i})| \qquad (4.4)$$

where t_i is an artificial variable created to represent each clause c_i that forms a CNF ϕ. Additionally, w_i represents the weight associated to clause c_i. So, the weighted MAX-SAT problem can be formulated as the integer program:

$$Min \sum_{\forall c_i \in C_\phi} w_i t_i \qquad (4.5)$$

Subject to: $\lambda(c_i)$ for all $c_i \in C_\phi$

Following, I shall briefly describe a translation of Lex^+ semantics to an integer programming problem.

4.3   A Mathematical Framework for Lex^+ Semantics

In this section, a translation ζ of a legal knowledge base Δ to a weighted MAX-SAT problem is proposed. This translation was introduced in Garcia and Brasil [2002c] regarding Pearl's System Z and in Garcia and Brasil [2002b] with respect to Lehmann's Lexicographic Closure. It was also applied to legal reasoning in Garcia and Brasil [2003]. I wish to thank Berilhes for allowing the use of such papers in the present dissertation. We also show the existing interrelationship among the solutions for this problem and the set of Lex^+ entailed legal consequences of Δ.

Informally, the main idea of the translation proposed in this work is that each conditional legal norm can be understood as a CNF, where each defeasible legal norm has a related specific weight (cost). The strict legal norms do not have a weight (cost), because they cannot be falsified. In other words, all strict norms ought to be satisfied. The objective function is to minimize the total cost of the sum of the unsatisfied CNF formula.

By δ_m^* we represent the material counterpart of the legal norm $\delta_m \in \Delta$. Moreover, by $CNF(\delta_m^*)$ we denote the CNF formula equivalent to δ_m^*. In addition, $B(H_{ci}) = P(H_{c_i}) \cup N(H_{c_i})$, definition 52, represents the set of binary variables associated to the clause $c_i \in CNF(\delta_m^*)$.

If the conditional δ_m is a defeasible legal norm $\alpha \to \beta$, then each clause $c_i \in CNF(\delta_m^*)$ will yield the following linear inequality:

$$\lambda(c_m) : \sum_{x_{a_k} \in P(H_{cm})} x_{a_k} \; - \sum_{x_{a_k} \in N(H_{cm})} x_{a_k} \; + t_m \geq 1 - |N(H_{cm})| \qquad (4.6)$$

Where t_m is a new binary variable, that does not appear in $B(H_{ci})$.

If the conditional δ_m is a strict legal norm $\alpha \Rightarrow \beta$, then each clause $c_i \in CNF(\delta_m^*)$ will generate the following linear inequality:

$$\lambda'(c_m) : \sum_{x_{a_k} \in P(H_{cm})} x_{a_k} \; - \sum_{x_{a_k} \in N(H_{cm})} x_{a_k} \; \geq 1 - |N(H_{cm})| \qquad (4.7)$$

The main difference among strict and defeasible legal norms is that we do not have a weight (cost) associated with strict norms, so the new binary variable t_m in the inequality linear system attributed to defeasible norms is not used.

Thus, the conditional legal norm δ_m yields the following linear inequalities system $(sd(\delta_m))$:

$$sd(\delta_m) = \begin{cases} \lambda(c_i) : \forall c_i \in CNF(\delta_m^*) \text{ iff } \delta_m \in D \\ \lambda'(c_i) : \forall c_i \in CNF(\delta_m^*) \text{ iff } \delta_m \in L \end{cases} \qquad (4.8)$$

A ζ-translation of the legal knowledge base Δ is defined as the union of the linear inequalities system generated by the translation of each legal norm belonging to Δ.

Definition 57 (ζ-translation of Δ) *The ζ-translation of Δ will be equal to the following linear inequalities system, $sd(\Delta)$:*

$$sd(\Delta) = \{sd(\delta_i) \mid \forall \delta_i \in \Delta\} \qquad (4.9)$$

■ **EXAMPLE 4.2**

The ζ-translation of Δ given by (3.7) is equal to the following system of linear inequalities $sd(\Delta)$:

$$sd(\Delta) = \begin{cases} & & t_1 & - & x_{fe} & - & x_w & \geq & -1 \\ & & t_2 & - & x_{fe} & - & x_{lt} & \geq & -1 \\ & & t_3 & - & x_d & + & x_{fe} & \geq & 0 \\ & & t_4 & - & x_d & + & x_{lt} & \geq & 0 \\ & & t_5 & - & x_l & + & x_w & \geq & 0 \\ & & & & x_d & - & x_l & \geq & 0 \\ & & & & x_d & - & x_{sl} & \geq & 0 \\ t_8 & - & x_r & - & x_{utv} & + & x_l & \geq & -1 \\ t_9 & - & x_p & - & x_{utv} & - & x_l & \geq & -2 \end{cases}$$

Next, an important element in formulating the weighted MAX-SAT problem is defined, that is, the appropriate weight of each clause in D.

The underlying idea is that more specific defeasible legal norms, i.e., those that belong to the higher order partition, should have priority over a less specific one. Hence, falsifying a more specific defeasible legal norm will result in a higher cost. Thus, the clauses generated from defeasible norms belonging to higher partitions of Lex^+ ought to have a higher cost, therefore the system will prefer to falsify a clause from a less specific legal norm than a more specific one.

Moreover, the Lex^+ semantics, definition 3.2.3, shows that it is preferable to falsify *all* legal norms that are less specific than a more specific one. Thus, the cost related to a defeasible norm $\delta_i \in D$ should be higher than the sum of the costs of all less specific ones. Finally, if two defeasible norms δ_p and δ_q are in conflict, but there is no preference relation among them, i.e., δ_p and δ_q belong to the same partition, then there is no preference in falsifying δ_p or δ_q. Note, however, that the Lex^+ semantics prefers to falsify only one of the conflicting defeasible legal norms, to avoid a contradiction.

Definition 58 (Cost Attribution) *A cost attribution $f(.)$ to the defeasible legal knowledge base D, is a mapping of elements from D to $\Re$.*

Definition 59 (Admissible Cost Attribution) *A cost attribution f is* admissible *wrt D iff the following conditions are satisfied:*

1. $f(\delta_m) > \sum\limits_{j<i} \sum\limits_{\delta_n \in D_j} f(\delta_n)$ for all $\delta_m \in D_i$

2. $f(\delta_m) = f(\delta_n)$ for all δ_m and δ_n belonging to the same partition of D.

The former constraint certifies that the cost of a defeasible norm δ_m will be higher than the sum of the costs of all less specific defeasible legal norms. The latter assures that all defeasible norms belonging to the same partition have the same cost.

⬛ EXAMPLE 4.3

An admissible cost attribution for example 3.7 is

$$10t_1 + 10t_2 + 100t_3 + 100t_4 + 100t_5 + 20t_8 + 10t_9$$

Definition 60 (MAX-SAT (Δ)) *Given a p-consistent Δ and an admissible cost attribution $f()$, we denote by MAX-SAT(Δ) the following combinatorial optimization problem:*

$$Min \sum f(\delta_i)\, t(\delta_i) \tag{4.10}$$

$$Subject\ to\ \ sd(\Delta)$$

Now, the main point consists in finding a relation, if one exists, among the solutions of the MAX-SAT problem described and the minimal interpretations with respect to Lex^+ semantics of Δ.

Initially we define the cost of an interpretation w as the sum of the individual costs of legal norms falsified by w.

Definition 61 (Cost of an interpretation) *The cost of an interpretation w wrt Δ is:*

$$V(w) = \sum_{\delta_i \in \overline{D}_w} f(\delta_i) \tag{4.11}$$

Where $\overline{D}_w$ is the set of defeasible norms falsified by w.

Definition 62 (Set of Clauses from Δ) *Given a legal knowledge base Δ, by $C(\Delta)$ we denote the set of clauses associated to Δ. And it is defined as follow:*

$$C(\Delta) = \{c_i | c_i \in CNF(\delta_m^*)\ for\ all\ \delta_m \in \Delta\} \tag{4.12}$$

Definition 63 (Binary variables of Δ) *If $B(\Delta)$ represents the set of binary variables associated to Δ, then it is defined as:*

$$B(\Delta) = \{x_a | x_a \in B(H_{c_i}),\ for\ all\ c_i \in C(\Delta)\} \tag{4.13}$$

Definition 64 (Variables Attribution) *Let w be an interpretation of Δ. The attribution of binary variables generated by w, that we denote by s_w, is defined as:*
for all $x_a \in B(\Delta)$:

$$s_w(x_a) = \begin{cases} 1 & if\ a\ is\ true\ in\ w \\ 0 & otherwise \end{cases} \tag{4.14}$$

for all variables t_i:

$$s_w(t_i) = \begin{cases} 1 & if\ \delta_i\ is\ falsified\ by\ w \\ 0 & otherwise \end{cases} \tag{4.15}$$

From an attribution of binary variables s_w generated by an interpretation w we can easily generate a solution for MAX-SAT(Δ):

Definition 65 *If u is a solution for a MAX-SAT(Δ) problem, then the interpretation generated by u, represented by w_u, is achieved adjusting the truth value of each literal a present in Δ to true iff $x_a = 1$ in u and adjusting the truth value of all other literals to false.*

Now, we can establish one of the main results of this work. Informally, the following theorem affirms that there exists a one-to-one correspondence between the solutions of a weighted MAX-SAT and the minimal interpretations of the legal knowledge base Δ wrt Lex^+ semantics.

Theorem 4.1 *u is an optimal solution to the MAX-SAT(Δ) problem (60) iff there exists a minimal interpretation m wrt a Lex^+ semantics of Δ, such that $s_m = u$ and $w_u = m$.*

Proof: If Part: Suppose that s_u is an optimal solution to the MAX-SAT(Δ) problem, so there exists no feasible solution with lower cost than s_u. To prove the *if* part we should prove that the interpretation generated by solution s_u (definition 65), represented by w_u, is a minimal interpretation with respect to the Lex^+ ordering of a conditional theory Δ. By contradiction, assume that w_u is not a minimal interpretation, then there exists an interpretation w_p, such that w_p is preferred to w_u, $w_p \prec w_u$. Therefore, according to definition 30, $\langle v_n(w_p), ..., v_0(w_p) \rangle < \langle v_n(w_u), ..., v_0(w_u) \rangle$. So, there exists an index k, such that $v_k(w_p) < v_k(w_u)$, and for all index i belonging to the interval $k < i \leq n$, we have $v_i(w_p) = v_i(w_u)$. Since the cost of a default δ that belongs to a partition of index k is greater than the sum of the costs of all defaults belonging to partitions of index lower than k, then the attribution of variables associated to the interpretation w_p, denoted by s_p, is a solution with cost strictly lower than s_u. Hence, s_u is not an optimal solution. Contradiction.

Only If Part: Suppose that w_r is a minimal interpretation with respect to the Lex^+ ordering; therefore, there exists no interpretation w_u such that $w_u \prec w_r$. To prove the only if part we should prove that the attribution of variables generated by interpretation w_r (definition 64), represented by s_r, is an optimal solution to the MAX-SAT(Δ) problem. By contradiction, assume that s_r is not an optimal solution to the MAX-SAT(Δ) problem, so there exists a solution s_p with cost lower than the cost s_p. The solution s_p can be converted in an interpretation, w_p, that is preferred to the interpretation w_r. Contradiction. ∎

Next, we define the notion of consensual applied to a defeasible legal norm δ_i : $\alpha \rightarrow \beta$ wrt a MAX-SAT problem(Δ).

Definition 66 *A legal norm $\delta_m : \alpha \rightarrow \beta$ is consensual wrt MAX-SAT(Δ) iff the cost of any optimal solution[2] of MAX-SAT(Δ) $\cup \{x_\alpha = 1, x_\beta = 1\}$ is smaller then the*

---

[2]Note that all optimal solution for a combinatorial optimization problem have the same cost.

cost of any optimal solution of MAX-SAT(Δ) $\cup \{x_\alpha = 1, x_\beta = 0\}$. If both costs are equal, then the defeasible legal norm $\delta_m : \alpha \to \beta$ is undecidable wrt Δ.

We shall introduce now the main results of this work. Informally, the first result says that a legal knowledge base Δ Lex^+ entails a legal norm $\delta_m : \alpha \to \beta$ iff this legal norm is consensual wrt combinatorial optimization problems resulting from the ζ-translation of $\Delta = (D, L)$.

Theorem 4.2 *A legal norm $\delta_m : \alpha \to \beta$ is Lex^+ entailed by a legal knowledge base Δ iff $\delta_m : \alpha \to \beta$ is consensual with respect to MAX-SAT(Δ) problem.*

Proof: If Part: Assume that $\delta_m : \alpha \to \beta$ is consensual with respect to MAX-SAT(Δ) problem, then there exists no optimal solution of MAX-SAT(Δ) $\cup \{x_\alpha = 1, x_\beta = 0\}$, with cost lower than the optimal solution of MAX-SAT(Δ) $\cup \{x_\alpha = 1, x_\beta = 1\}$. To prove the *if* part we should prove that δ_m is Lex^+ entailed by a conditional knowledge base Δ. By contradiction, assume that δ_m is not Lex^+ entailed by Δ, then the interpretation w_u that satisfies α and β is not preferred, i.e., there exists an interpretation w_p such that $w_p \prec w_u$, where $w_p = \alpha \wedge \neg\beta$ and $w_u = \alpha \wedge \beta$. According to definition 30, $w_p \prec w_u$ iff $\langle v_n(w_p), ..., v_0(w_p) \rangle < \langle v_n(w_u), ..., v_0(w_u) \rangle$, that is, the number of defaults falsified by w_p is lower than the number of defaults falsified by w_u. Hence, there exists an index k, such that $v_k(w_p) < v_k(w_u)$, and for all index i belonging to the interval $k < i \le n$, we have $v_i(w_p) = v_i(w_u)$. Since the cost of a defeasible conditional δ_m that belongs to a partition of index k is greater than the sum of the costs of all defaults belonging to partitions of index lower than k, then the attribution of variables associated to the interpretation w_p yields an optimal solution of MAX-SAT(Δ) $\cup \{x_\alpha = 1, x_\beta = 0\}$, with cost lower than any optimal solution of MAX-SAT(Δ) $\cup \{x_\alpha = 1, x_\beta = 1\}$. Therefore, δ_m is not consensual. Contradiction.

Only If Part: Assume that $\delta_m : \alpha \to \beta$ is Lex^+ entailed by a conditional knowledge base Δ, and w_u is a minimal interpretation wrt the Lex^+ ordering. Then there exists no interpretation w_p such that $w_p \prec w_u$. To prove the only if part we should prove that δ_m is consensual wrt MAX-SAT(Δ) problem, that is, the cost of any optimal solution of MAX-SAT(Δ) $\cup \{x_\alpha = 1, x_\beta = 1\}$ is lower than the cost of any optimal solution of MAX-SAT(Δ) $\cup \{x_\alpha = 1, x_\beta = 0\}$. By contradiction, assume that δ_m is not consensual wrt MAX-SAT(Δ) problem. Hence, there exists an $\delta_n : \alpha \to \neg\beta$ such that the cost of any optimal solution of MAX-SAT(Δ) $\cup \{x_\alpha = 1, x_\beta = 0\}$ is strictly lower than the cost of MAX-SAT(Δ) $\cup \{x_\alpha = 1, x_\beta = 1\}$. Since δ_n yields a feasible solution with cost lower than δ_m, then the number of defaults falsified by an interpretation w_p of δ_n is lower than the number of defaults falsified by w_u of δ_m, that is, $v_k(w_p) < v_k(w_u)$, for some index k, and $v_i(w_p) = v_i(w_u)$, for some $k < i \le n$. According to definition 31, w_p is preferred to w_u, $w_p \prec w_u$, iff $\langle v_n(w_p), ..., v_0(w_p) \rangle < \langle v_n(w_u), ..., v_0(w_u) \rangle$. Therefore, w_u is not a minimal interpretation wrt the Lex^+-ordering and δ_m is not Lex^+ entailed by Δ. Contradiction. ∎

We can now derive a legal norm or a legal argument from a legal knowledge base Δ. But we also want to derive a judicial decision ψ from Δ whenever an evidence ϕ is known. This feature can be simply obtained by the *deduction theorem* in propositional calculus:

Theorem 4.3 (Deduction Theorem Kleene [1952]) *For the propositional calculus, if* $\Gamma, \sigma \vdash \tau$, *then* $\Gamma \vdash \sigma \supset \tau$

Proof: This theorem is the first for propositional calculus and the proof can be easily found in the literature. For all, see [Kleene, 1952, pp. 90].   ■

We can apply this theorem to legal reasoning modeled under Lex^+ closure in the following:

Theorem 4.4 *A judicial decision* ψ *is* Lex^+ *entailed by a legal knowledge base* Δ *and a literal* ϕ, *denoted by* $\Delta \cup \{\phi\} \mathrel{\vert\!\sim} \psi$, *iff* $\Delta \mathrel{\vert\!\sim} \phi \rightarrow \psi$.

Proof: The proof is quite straightforward from the if-then-elimination and or-elimination.

$$\Delta \mathrel{\vert\!\sim} \phi \rightarrow \psi$$
$$\Delta \mathrel{\vert\!\sim} \neg\phi \vee \psi$$
$$\Delta, \phi \mathrel{\vert\!\sim} \psi$$

■

We shall define now the concept of consentaneous, that actually follows from definition 66 and theorem 4.4:

Definition 67 *A judicial decision* ψ *is consentaneous wrt MAX-SAT(Δ)* $\cup\{x_\phi = 1\}$ *iff the cost of any optimal solution of MAX-SAT(Δ)* $\cup\{x_\phi = 1, x_\psi = 1\}$ *is lower than the cost of any optimal solution of MAX-SAT(Δ)* $\cup\{x_\phi = 1, x_\psi = 0\}$. *If both costs are equal, then* ψ *is undecidable wrt* $\Delta \cup \{\phi\}$.

Theorem 4.5 *A judicial decision* ψ *is* Lex^+ *entailed by* $\Delta \cup \{\phi\}$ *iff* ψ *is consentaneous with respect to MAX-SAT(Δ)* $\cup\{x_\phi = 1\}$.

Proof: If Part: Assume that ψ is consentaneous wrt MAX-SAT(Δ) $\cup\{x_\phi = 1\}$, then there exists no optimal solution of MAX-SAT(Δ) $\cup\{x_\phi = 1, x_\psi = 0\}$ with costs lower than optimal solution of MAX-SAT(Δ) $\cup\{x_\phi = 1, x_\psi = 1\}$. To prove the if part we should prove that ψ is Lex^+ entailed by a legal knowledge base Δ and an evidence ϕ, $\Delta \cup \{\phi\} \mathrel{\vert\!\sim} \psi$. According to definition 4.4, ψ is Lex^+ entailed by $\Delta \cup \{\phi\}$ iff $\Delta \mathrel{\vert\!\sim} \delta_m : \phi \rightarrow \psi$. By contradiction, assume that ψ is not Lex^+ entailed by $\Delta \cup \{\phi\}$ which also means that Δ does not Lex^+ entail a default $\delta_m : \phi \rightarrow \psi$. So, the interpretation w_u that satisfies ϕ and ψ is not preferred, i.e., there exists an interpretation w_p such that $w_p \prec w_u$, where $w_p = \phi \wedge \neg\psi$ and $w_u = \phi \wedge \psi$. Since $w_p \prec w_u$ iff $\langle v_n(w_p), ..., v_0(w_p) \rangle < \langle v_n(w_u), ..., v_0(w_u) \rangle$, then $v_k(w_p) < v_k(w_u)$ for some index k, and $v_i(w_p) = v_i(w_u)$ for some $k < i \leq n$. Notice that the cost of a default δ_m that belongs to a partition of index k is greater than the sum of the costs of all defaults belonging to partitions of index lower than k. Consequently, the attribution of variables associated to the interpretation w_p yields an optimal solution of MAX-SAT(Δ) $\cup\{x_\phi = 1, x_\psi = 0\}$ with cost lower than any optimal solution of MAX-SAT(Δ) $\cup\{x_\phi = 1, x_\psi = 1\}$. Therefore, ψ is not consentaneous wrt MAX-SAT(Δ) $\cup\{x_\phi = 1\}$. Contradiction.

Only If Part: Assume that ψ is Lex^+ entailed by $\Delta \cup \{\phi\}$, which means that $\Delta|\sim \delta_m : \phi \rightarrow \psi$, and that w_u is a minimal interpretation wrt the Lex^+ ordering. Then, there exists no interpretation w_p such that $w_p \prec w_u$. To prove the only if part we should prove that ψ is consentaneous wrt MAX-SAT(Δ) $\cup\{x_\phi = 1\}$, see definition 67. By contradiction, assume that ψ is not consentaneous wrt MAX-SAT(Δ) $\cup\{x_\phi = 1\}$. Hence, the cost of any optimal solution of MAX-SAT(Δ) $\cup\{x_\phi = 1, x_\psi = 0\}$ is lower than the cost of any optimal solution of MAX-SAT(Δ) $\cup\{x_\phi = 1, x_\psi = 1\}$. The optimal solution of MAX-SAT(Δ) $\cup\{x_\phi = 1, x_\psi = 0\}$ is generated from the attribution of variables associated to the interpretation $w_p = \phi \wedge \neg\psi$, for some $\delta_n : \phi \rightarrow \neg\psi$. In other words, δ_n yields a feasible solution with costs lower than δ_m, and thus the number of defaults falsified by an interpretation w_p of δ_n is lower than the number of defaults falsified by w_u of δ_m, that is, $v_k(w_p) < v_k(w_u)$ for some index k, and $v_i(w_p) = v_i(w_u)$ for some $k < i \leq n$. Since w_p is preferred to w_u iff $\langle v_n(w_p), ..., v_0(w_p)\rangle < \langle v_n(w_u), ..., v_0(w_u)\rangle$ then w_u is not a minimal interpretation wrt the Lex^+ ordering and Δ does not Lex^+ entail $\delta_m : \phi \rightarrow \psi$. Therefore, ψ is not Lex^+ entailed by $\Delta \cup \{\phi\}$. Contradiction. ∎

The following algorithm can determine if a judicial decision ψ is Lex^+ entailed by $\Delta = (D, L) \cup \{\phi\}$.

.

Algorithm
Input: a Lex^+-consistent $\Delta = (D, L)$, an evidence ϕ and a judicial decision ψ;

Output: Yes, if $\Delta \cup \{\phi\}\!\!\sim \psi$. No, otherwise.

1. Build the optimization problems MAX-SAT(Δ) $\cup\{x_\phi = 1, x_\psi = 1\}$ and MAX-SAT(Δ) $\cup\{x_\phi = 1, x_\psi = 0\}$.

2. Solve these problems using one of the algorithms for integer programming. Let c and c' be the cost of optimal solutions of the first and second problems, respectively.

3. If $c < c'$ then return yes else return no

The theorems 4.2 and 4.5 are in the core of this algorithm.

▉ EXAMPLE 4.4

Consider the legal knowledge base Δ given in example 3.7. As long as we know the evidence sl (John Doe is a slanderer), we want to know whether $\Delta \cup \{sl\}$ Lex^+ entails a judicial decision lt (John Doe ought to be liable in tort). For simplicity, we shall only consider the most normal worlds wrt sl, that is, $w_u = \{sl, fe, d\}$ and $w_v = \{sl, fe, d, lt\}$. From the attribution of binary variables, we thus have the following models M' of w_u and $M^\star$ of w_v:

$$M' = \begin{cases} x_{fe} = 1 \\ x_{sl} = 1 \\ x_d = 1 \\ x_w = 0 \\ x_{lt} = 0 \end{cases} \quad M^\star = \begin{cases} x_{fe} = 1 \\ x_{sl} = 1 \\ x_d = 1 \\ x_w = 0 \\ x_{lt} = 1 \end{cases}$$

Since M' falsifies $\delta_4 : d \to lt$, then the artificial variable t_4 is forced to 1 to satisfy the clause $t_4 - x_d + x_{lt} \geq 0$, and since $M^\star$ falsifies $\delta_2 : fe \to \neg lt$, then the artificial variable t_2 is forced to 1 to satisfy the clause $t_2 - x_{fe} - x_{lt} \geq -1$. Therefore, the artificial variables t_i of each model has the following values:

$$M' = \begin{cases} t_1 = 0 \\ t_2 = 0 \\ t_3 = 0 \\ t_4 = 1 \\ t_5 = 0 \end{cases} \quad M^\star = \begin{cases} t_1 = 0 \\ t_2 = 1 \\ t_3 = 0 \\ t_4 = 0 \\ t_5 = 0 \end{cases}$$

An admissible cost attribution of example 3.7 (viz. 4.3) is:

$$10t_1 + 10t_2 + 100t_3 + 100t_4 + 100t_5 + 20t_8 + 10t_9$$

which yields to each model the following costs:

$$M' = 100$$
$$M^\star = 10$$

Since $M^\star < M'$ then $M^\star$ is preferred, and lt is consentaneous wrt MAX-SAT(Δ) $\cup \{x_{sl} = 1\}$. Therefore, $\Delta \cup \{sl\} \hspace{-0.2em}\mid\hspace{-0.55em}\sim lt$, that is, the judicial decision lt (John ought to be convicted for tort liability) is entailed.

4.4 Tractability of Conditional Logics

In this section, I shall make only some references about the tractability problem, rather then analysing it. The interested reader should see the referred papers.

The tractability problem of conditional logics is twofold. First, we have to compute the ordering of the conditional knowledge base (partitioning upon Z^+-ordering for Lex^+ Semantics). Second, the computation of an arbitrary query which is based on checking the models to verify whether an outcome is entailed or not.

The first complexity issue, i.e., the computation of Z^+ ranking of a consistent $\Delta^+ = \{\delta_i | \delta_i = \phi_i \xrightarrow{\sigma_i} \psi_i\}$, requires $O(n^2 \times \log n)$ satisfiability tests. This theorem of Goldszmidt and Pearl was proved on Goldszmidt and Pearl [1996]. Although it may seem surprising the complexity of the ordering, since Z^+ ranking is manipulating worlds, one should note that actually the procedure computes the *rules* in RZ^+

instead of *worlds*. The algorithm is written is this way by Goldszmidt and Pearl to show the connection with the equations given by definition 3.5 of Chapter 3.

The second tractability problem is usually hopeless. In general case, conditional logics are intractable, as long as the query manipulates worlds which number grow exponentially. However, there are some special cases where conditional logics are tractable allowing the development of efficient implementations. Eiter and Lukasiewicz have introduced in Eiter and Lukasiewicz [2000] two tractable classes, respectively *q-Horn* and *ff-Horn*. In *q-Horn* conditional knowledge bases, the Horn conditional knowledge bases are syntactically generalized by allowing a restricted form of disjunction, whilst in *ff-Horn* (*feedback-free Horn*) the interaction of the conditionals among each other must be controlled such that interferences have local effects. Another work of interest is the paper of Garcia [2003]. In this truly remarkable work, Garcia introduced two new tractable classes for default reasoning. The first class is the *nc-knowledge base* (*nested conditional knowledge base*), which is mainly based on the concept of nested class presented by Knuth [1990] and the second one is the *co-nc-knowledge base* (*co-nested conditional knowledge base*), which represents the dual of the first class and is based on the concepts of Co-Nested formulas introduced by Kratochvíl and Krivánek [1993].

CHAPTER 5

CONCLUSION

K υκνειον   ασμα
(*Swan's chant*)

—Diogenes 5,37

Related Research. As long as legal reasoning is characterized by uncertainty (incomplete and inconsistent information), it is natural to look for a logical framework to solve the inference problem in law on nonmonotonic literature. Several nonmonotonic formalisms for legal reasoning have been proposed, as well some implementations. There have been a few proposals to instantiate nonmonotonic reasoning as an Integer Programming too, all of them addressing the implementation of logic programming and none was translated to legal reasoning. As far as I know, this is the first time it is proposed. An important work was done by Bell *et al.* [1994], who described an implementation of the declarative semantics of both explicit and nonmonotonic negation in logic programs. Another work was from Kagan *et al.* [1994], which uses partial instantiation to compute all the consequences of a first order logic program, not necessarily ground. In Simons [1997], an algorithm was introduced for computing the stable models of ground logic programs, i.e., inferable from purely negative assumptions, which are derived from autoepistemic logic. However, their frameworks differs from ours, since we use Lehmann's lexicographic closure as the underlying semantics for legal reasoning, rather then logic programming. We also use a *weighted* MAX-SAT, to allow ranking and the lexicographic closure of a legal knowledge base, which results in a different inequality system from those described in the literature.

We should note that much attention has been paid to nonmonotonic formalisms for representing legal reasoning, in particular, variants of logic programming and a huge amount of recent work on argumentation systems. To acknowledge but a few of this body of work, we can cite the following. Gordon [1993a] formalizes legal reasoning in Conditional Entailment based on Alexy's Theory. Notice that the mathematical programming structure presented in this work can benefit from the argumentation framework of Gordon [1993a]. There also have been the works of Prakken [1997], Hage [1997], Verheij [1996], Sartor [1994], Branting [2000], Bench-Capon and Sergot [1985], Prakken and Vreeswijk [2002], to name but a few, regarding legal reasoning as argumentation systems. Most of these works are based on variants of logic programming, and although there exists a translation of logic programming to MAX-SAT, the translation of the cited legal reasoning formalisms to a mathematical programming framework remains to be investigated. Notice that there has been renewed interest in the use of SAT solvers as the core of inference systems, and we believe that this could be a very practical method to solve legal reasoning inference problem.

Conclusion. This dissertation addressed three main contributions: (i) a sound and complete logical model for legal reasoning, including a framework for weighing and balancing; (ii) an extension of Lehmann's Lexicographic Closure regarding variable strength conditionals, which we have called Lex^+ Semantics; and (iii) a ζ-translation of the semantics to a Weighted MAX-SAT problem, to allow its implementation in a mathematical framework. Actually, the results was connected with the main problem: how to compute legal reasoning through conditional logics. It was necessary to extend the Lehmann's Lexicographic Closure to the Lex^+ semantics in order to capture legal reasoning patterns, before the translation to MAX-SAT. Thus, the inference problem in legal knowledge bases can be treated as a combinatorial optimization problem, specifically through a weighted MAX-SAT model. For each legal knowledge base a family of weighted MAX-SAT problems is defined in such a way that there exists a one-to-one relation between the optimal solutions of each one of these problems and the minimal models obtained by lexicographic closure of the respective legal knowledge base.

At first sight, rewriting inference problems in legal knowledge bases as combinatorial optimization problems may be seen as trying to make a hard problem even more difficult, since integer programming problems are known as hard solving problems. However, three issues make us believe that this approach deserves attention:

First, it allows the development of solid implementations, based on algorithms and linear integer programming systems, to several semantics of legal knowledge bases. Note that in this dissertation, we introduced only a ζ-translation to the Lex^+ Semantics.

Second, recent results of Eiter and Lukasiewicz [2000] have shown that the logical inference problem on conditional knowledge bases under various semantics, among them the lexicographic semantics, is in general intractable. We believe that heuristics and approximation algorithms to MAX-SAT problem can be used to by-pass this obstacle.

And finally, there are many integer programs that can be easily solved in polynomial time once a special mathematical structure has been detected in the model, extending, therefore, the tractable classes of problems. In Garcia [2003], two new tractable classes of default reasoning over conditional knowledge bases were introduced, and can be used to solve the tractability problem of the inference relation in legal knowledge bases.

Future Works. The research over the subject matter is not finished. There are several open problems. A problem that remains to be investigated is the coherence in law under the Lex^+ System and the ζ-translation. So, a future research will demonstrate whether the translation allow high degrees of coherence, as discussed in Peczenik [1989]. Another issue that remains opened is the full comparison of the results of weighing proposed in this dissertation with Alexy's Balancing Theory. Although I have used sometimes the double-triadic method of Alexy [2003], the calculus are of different kind, and can produce different results. Specially when the Lex^+ is applied to the variable strength conditional instead of the double-triadic method. An important problem that claims for a detailed research is the development of an argumentation framework for the semantics introduced in this paper. Since legal reasoning is primarily oriented toward a logic of obligation, a modal deontic extension to the theory is also a subject for future research. Regarding the computational issues, it should be investigated whether the tractable classes proposed by the literature yield the expected results of legal reasoning and practical argumentation.

Bibliography

Aulis Aarnio, Robert Alexy, and Aleksander Peczenik. The foundation of legal reasoning. *Rechtstheorie*, 12:133–158, 257–279, 423–448, 1981.

Aulis Aarnio. *The Rational as Reasonable. A Treatise of Legal Justification.* Dordrecht/Boston/Lancaster/Tokyo: Reidel, 1987.

E. W. Adams. *The Logic of Conditionals.* D. Reidel, Dordrecht, Netherlands, 1975.

J. M. Adeodato. The rethorical syllogism (enthymeme) in judicial argumentation. *Paper presented at IVR-99 World Congress on Philosophy of Law and Social Philosophy, New York, 1999.*

C. E. Alchourrón and E. Bulygin. *Normative Systems.* Wien-New York: Springer Verlag, 1971.

C. E. Alchourrón and E. Bulygin. Unvollständigkeit, widersprüchlichkeit und unbestimmtheit der normenordnungen. *Deontische Logik und Semantik*, pages 20–32, 1977.

C. E. Alchourrón and D. Makinson. Hierarchies of regulations and their logic. *New Studies in Deontic Logic.*, pages 125–148, 1981.

C.E. Alchourrón, P. Gardenfors, and D. Makinson. On the logic of theory change: Partial meet functions for contraction and revision. *Journal of Symbolic Logic*, 50:510–530, 1985.

C. E. Alchourrón. Philophical foundations of deontic logic and the logic of defeasible conditionals. *Deontic Logic in Computer Science*, pages 43–84, 1993.

R. Alexy. *Theorie der juristischen Argumentation. Die Theorie des rationalen Diskurses als eine Theorie der juristischen Begründung*. Frankfurt am Main: Suhrkamp Verlag, 1978.

R. Alexy. *Theorie der Grundrechte*. Baden-Baden: Nomos, 1985.

R. Alexy. *Begriff und Geltung des Rechts*. Verlag Karl Alber GmbH, Freiburg/München, 1994.

R. Alexy. On balancing and subsumption. a structural comparision. *Ratio Juris (forthcoming)*, 2003.

N. D. Andrejew and D. A. Kerimow. Über die verwendungsmöglichkeiten der kybernetik bei der lösung juristischer probleme. *Voprosy Filosofii, Moscau*, page 106 f., 1960.

K.D. Ashley and E.L. Rissland. But, see, accord: Generating blue book citations in HYPO. *Proceedings of the First International Conference on Artificial Intelligence and Law*, pages 67–74, 1987.

M. Atienza. *Sobre la Analogia en el Derecho. Ensayo de Análisis de un razonamiento juridico*. Editorial Civitas S.A., Madrid, 1986.

G. Baumgärtel. Rechtstatsachen zur dauer des zivilprozesses. *Prozeßrechtliche Abhandlungen*, 1972.

J. R. S. Bedaque. *Direito e Processo. Influência do Direito Material sobre o Processo*. São Paulo: Malheiros, 2001.

Colin Bell, Anil Nerode, Raymond T. Ng, and V. S. Subrahmanian. Mixed integer programming methods for computing nonmonotonic deductive databases. *Journal of the ACM*, 41(6):1178–1215, 1994.

Colin Bell, Anil Nerode, Raymond T. Ng, and V. S. Subrahmanian. Implementing deductive databases by mixed integer programming. *ACM Transactions on Database Systems*, 21(2):238–269, 1996.

T. J. M. Bench-Capon and M. J. Sergot. Towards a rule-based representation of open texture in law. *Computing Power and Legal Reasoning*, pages 39–60, 1985.

S. Benferhat, C. Cayrol, D. Dubois, J. Lang, and H. Prade. Inconsistency management and prioritized syntax-base entailment. *Proc. 13th International Joint Conference on Artificial Intelligence (IJCAI-93)*, pages 640–645, 1993.

Ernest Rudolf Bierling. *Juristische Prinzipienlehre.* vol. I, 1894; vol. II, 1898; vol. III, 1905; vol. IV, 1911; vol. V, 1917, full ed. 1961, Freiburg i. Br. and Leipzig: J.C.B. Mohr, repr. Aalen: Scientia, 1979.

Norberto Bobbio. *Teoria dell'ordinamento giuridico.* Editore G. Giappichelli, 1982.

R. A. Bourne and S. Parsons. Maximum entropy and variable strength defaults. *Proc. 16th International Joint Conference on Artificial Intelligence (IJCAI-99),* pages 50–55, 1999.

R. A. Bourne. *Default Reasoning using Maximum Entropy and Variable Strength Defaults.* PhD Thesis. University of London, 1999.

L. Karl Branting. *Reasoning with Rules and Precedents. A Computational Model of Legal Analysis.* Revised Ph.D. Dissertation (1991), Dordrecht-Boston-London: Kluwer Academic Publishers, 2000.

Samuel M. Brasil and Berilhes B. Garcia. Modelling legal reasoning in a mathematical environment through model theoretic semantics. *ICAIL 03,* 2003.

Gerhard Brewka, Jürgen Dix, and Kurt Konolige. *Nonmonotonic Reasoning: An Overview.* CSLI Publications, 1997.

G. Brewka. Cumulative default logic: in defense of nonmonotonic inference rules. *Artificial Intelligence,* 50:183–205, 1991.

G. Brewka. Adding priorities and specificity to default logic. *JELIA'94, LNAI 838, Springer, Berlin,* pages 247–260, 1994.

G. Brewka. Reasoning about priorities in default logic. *Proceedings of AAAI-94,* pages 940–945, 1994.

B.G. Buchanan and T.E. Headrick. Some speculation about artificial intelligence and legal reasoning. *Stanford Law Review,* 23:40–62, 1970.

H. P. Bull. Automation in der verwaltung? *Juristische Rundschau,* page 178 f., 1965.

Eugenio Bulygin. On legal gaps. *Paper presented at IVR-03 World Congress on Philosophy of Law and Social Philosophy, Lund,* 2003.

V. Chandru and J. N. Hooker. *Optimization Methods for Logical Inference.* Series in Discrete Mathematics and Optimization. John Wiley & Sons, Inc., 1999.

Brian F. Chellas. *Modal Logic. An Introduction.* Cambridge University Press, Cambridge, 1980.

Alonzo Church. *Introduction to Mathematical Logic.* Princeton University Press, Princeton, New Jersey, 1956.

K. Clark. Negation as failure. *Logic and Data Bases,* 1978.

Edward Coke. *The Institutes of the Laws of England*. London: W. Clarke and Sons, 1817.

Stephen A. Cook. The complexity of theorem-proving procedures. In *ACM Symposium on Theory of Computing*, pages 151–158, 1971.

I.M. Copi. *Introduction to Logic*. New York: Macmillan, 1961.

Oscar Correas. *Crítica da Ideologia Jurídica. Ensaio Sócio-Semiológico*. Porto Alegre: Sérgio Antonio Fabris Editor, 1995.

Haskell B. Curry. *Foundations of Mathematical Logic*. New York: Dover Publications, Inc., 1977.

T. Dean and D. McDermott. Temporal data base management. *Artificial Intelligence*, 32:1–55, 1987.

C. R. Dinamarco. Relativizar a coisa julgada. *REPRO - Revista de Processo*, 109, 2003.

J. Doyle. A truth maintenance system. *Artificial Intelligence*, 12:231–272, 1979.

D. Dubois and H. Prade. *Possibility Theory. An Approach to the Computerized Processing of Uncertainty*. New York: Plenum Press, 1988.

Ronald Dworkin. Is law a system of rules? *Reprinted in The Philosophy of Law*, pages 38–65, 1967.

Ronald Dworkin. *Taking Rights Seriously*. Cambridge: Harvard University Press, 1977.

Thomas Eiter and Thomas Lukasiewicz. Default reasoning from conditional knowledge bases: Complexity and tractable cases. *Artificial Intelligence*, 124(2):169–241, 2000.

D. W. Etherington. Formalizing nonmonotonic reasoning systems. *Artificial Intelligence*, 31:41–85, 1987.

H. Fiedler. Rechenautomaten als hilfsmittel der gesetzesanwendung. *Deutsche Rentenversicherung*, page 149 f., 1962.

H. Fiedler. Probleme der elektronischen datenverarbeitung in der öffentlichen verwaltung. *Deutsche Rentenversicherung*, page 40 f., 1964.

H. Fiedler. Rechenautomaten in recht und verwaltung. *JZ*, page 689 f., 1966.

H. Fiedler. Computer für die justiz. *JZ*, pages 556–557, 1968.

J. Frank. *Courts on Trial*. Princeton University Press, 1949.

Berilhes B. Garcia and Samuel M. Brasil. Towards default reasoning through maxsat. *SBIA 2002 LNAI, Springer-Verlag: Berlin Heidelberg*, 2507:52–62, 2002.

Berilhes Borges Garcia and Samuel Meira Brasil, Jr. Reasoning from conditional knowledge bases through mathematical programming. 2002.

Berilhes Borges Garcia and Samuel Meira Brasil, Jr. Towards default reasoning through MAX-SAT. *Lecture Notes in Computer Science*, 2507:52–62, 2002.

Berilhes Borges Garcia and Samuel Meira Brasil, Jr. Modelling legal reasoning in a mathematical environment through model theoretic semantics. *Proceedings of the ICAIL-03 - International Conference of Artificial Intelligence and Law, Edinburgh*, pages 195–203, 2003.

D. S. Garcia. *Introdução à Informática Jurídica*. São Paulo, Bushatsky, Ed. da Universidade de São Paulo, 1976.

Berilhes Borges Garcia. New tractable classes for default reasoning from conditional knowledge bases. *to appear*, 2003.

Hector Geffner and Judea Pearl. Conditional entailment: bridging two approaches to default reasoning. *Artificial Intelligence*, 53:209–244, 1992.

Hector Geffner. *Default Reasoning: Causal and Conditional Theories*. MIT Press, Cambridge, MA, 1992.

Theodor Geiger. *Vorstudien zu einer Soziologie des Rechts*. Manfred Rehbinder, 1947.

Moises Goldszmidt and Judea Pearl. On the consistency of defeasible databases. *Artificial Intelligence*, 52(2):121–149, 1991.

Moises Goldszmidt and Judea Pearl. System z^+: A formalism for reasoning with variable strength defaults. *Proceedings 9th National Conference on Artificial Intelligence (AAAI-91)*, pages 399–404, 1991. Anaheim, CA.

Moises Goldszmidt and Judea Pearl. Rank-based systems: A simple approach to belief revision, belief update, and reasoning about evidence and actions. *Proceedings of the Third International Conference on Principles of Knowledge Representation and Reasoning*, 1992.

Moisés Goldszmidt and Judea Pearl. Qualitative probabilities for default reasoning, belief revision, and causal modeling. *Artificial Intelligence*, 84:57–112, 1996.

M. Goldszmidt, P. Morris, and J. Pearl. A maximum entropy approach to nonmonotonic reasoning. *IEEE Transactions on Pattern Analysis and Machine Intelligence*, 15(3):220–232, 1993.

T.F. Gordon and N. Karacapilidis. The zeno argumentation framework. *Proceedings of the 6th International Conference on Artificial Intelligence and Law*, 1997.

T.F. Gordon. The pleadings game - an artificial intelligence model of procedural justice. *Dissertation*, 1993.

T.F. Gordon. The pleadings game - formalizing procedural justice. *Proceedings of the 4th International Conference on Artificial Intelligence and Law*, 1993.

Jun Gu, Paul W. Purdom, John Franco, and Benjamin W. Wah. Algorithms for the satisfiability (SAT) problem: a survey. In Dingzhu Du, Jun Gu, and Panos M. Pardalos, editors, *Satisfiability Problem: Theory and Applications*, volume 35 of *DIMACS: Series in Discrete Mathematics and Theoretical Computer Science*, pages 19–152. American Mathematical Society, 1997.

Kurt Gödel. Russell's mathematical logic. *Schilpp*, pages 123–153, 1944. reprinted in Gödel Collected Works, Oxford University Press, 1986.

Susan Haack. *Deviant Logic*. University of Chicago Press, Chicago, 1996.

Jaap C. Hage. *Reasoning with Rules. An Essay on Legal Reasoning and Its Underlying Logic*. Dordrecht-Boston-London: Kluwer Academic Publishers, 1997.

T. Hailperin. *Boole's Logic and Probability: A Critical Exposition from Standpoint of Contemporary Algebra and Probability Theory*. North Holland, Amsterdam, 1976.

S. Hanks and D. McDermott. Temporal reasoning and default logics. *Technical report*, 1985.

H. L. A. Hart. The ascription of responsability and rights. *Proceedings of the Aristotelean Society*, 49, p. 171-194, (1949):145–166, 1949.

H. L. A. Hart. Positivism and the separation of law and morals. *Harvard Law Review*, 71, 593-629:17–37, 1958.

Herbert L. A. Hart. *The Concept of Law*. Oxford: Clarendon Press, 1961.

Peter Hay. *Law of the United States: An overview*. München: Beck, 2002.

J. Hintikka. Some main problems of deontic logic. *Deontic Logic: Introductory and Systematic Readings*, 1971. Dordrecht e.a.

Thomas Hobbes. *Dialogue Between a Philosopher and a Student of the Common Laws of England*. Chicago: University of Chicago Press, 1971.

W. N. Hohfeld. *Fundamental Legal Conceptions as applied to Legal Reasoning*. New Haven, Connecticut: Yale University Press, 1923.

John N. Hooker. A quantitative approach to logical inference. *Decision Support Systems*, 4:45–69, 1988.

D. Hunter. Maximum entropy updating and conditionalization. *Existence and Explanation. Essays in Honor of Karel Lambert*, Dordrecht: Kluwer Academic Publishers:45–57, 1991.

Axel Anders Hägerström. *Inquiries into the Nature of Law and Morals.* Stockholm: Almqvist and Wiksell, 1953.

R. C. Jeffrey. *The Logic of Decision.* University of Chicago Press, 1965. Chicago, 2. Aufl. 1983.

Robert G. Jeroslow. *Logic-Based Decision Support. Mixed Integer Model Formulation.* Elsevier, Amsterdam, 1988.

Vadim Kagan, Anil Nerode, and V. S. Subrahmanian. Computing definite logic programs by partial instantiation. *Annals of Pure and Applied Logic,* 67(1-3):161–182, 1994.

Wilhelm Kamlah and Paul Lorenzen. *Logische Propädeutik: Vorschule des vernünftigen Redens.* Mannheim: Bibliographisches Institut AG, 1973.

Mary Kay Kane. *Civil Procedure.* St. Paul (Minn.): West Publishing, 1993.

Hans Kelsen. *Reine Rechtslehre. Einleitung in die rechtswissenschaftliche Problematik.* Vienna: Franz Deuticke, 1934.

Hans Kelsen. *Reine Rechtslehre.* Vien: Verlag Franz Deuticke, 1960.

Stephen Cole Kleene. *Introduction to Metamathematics.* Groningen: Wolters-Noordhoff Publishing, Amsterdam: North-Holland Publishing Company, 1952.

Ulrich Klug and H. Fiedler. Die berucksichtigung der automatisierten gesetzesausführung in der gesetzgebung. *Deutsche Rentenversicherung,* page 269 f., 1964.

Ulrich Klug. *Juristische Logik.* Berlin - Heidelberg: Springer Verlag, 1966.

Viktor Knapp. De l'application de la cybernetique au domaine du droit. *Revue de Droit Contemporain, Bruxelas,* page 13/34, 1963.

D. E. Knuth. Nested satisfiability. *Acta Informatica,* 28(1):1–6, 1990.

R. A. Kowalski and M. J. Sergot. A logic-based calculus of events. *New Generation Computing,* 4:67–95, 1986.

J. Kratochvíl and M. Krivánek. Satisfiability of co-nested formulas. *Acta Informatica,* 30(4):397–403, 1993.

S. Kraus, D. Lehmann, and M. Magidor. Nonmonotonic reasoning, preferential models and cumulative logics. *Artificial Intelligence,* 44:167–207, 1990.

D. Lehmann and M. Magidor. Rational logics and their models: A study in cumulative logics. *Technical Report TR-88-16, Dept. of Computer Science, Hebrew University, Jerusalem, Israel,* 1988.

D. Lehmann and M. Magidor. What does a conditional knowledge base entail? *Artificial Intelligence*, 55:1–60, 1992.

Daniel Lehmann. Another perspective on default reasoning. *Annals of Mathematics and Artificial Intelligence*, 15(1):61–82, 1995.

Vladimir Lifschitz. Pointwise circumscription: Preliminary report. *Proceedings of the Conference of the American Association of Artificial Intelligence*, Philadelphia, PA:406–410, 1986.

Vladimir Lifschitz. Circumscription. *Handbook of Logic in Artificial Intelligence and Logic Programming - Nonmonotonic and Uncertain Reasoning*, 3:297–352, 1994.

L. Lindahl. *Position and Change*. Dordrecht: Reidel, 1977.

A.R. Lodder and A. Herczog. Dialaw - a dialogical framework for modeling legal reasoning. *Proceedings of the 5th International Conference on Artificial Intelligence and Law*, pages 146–155, 1995.

Arno R. Lodder. *DiaLaw. On Legal Justification and Dialogical Models of Argumentation*. Dordrecht/Boston/London: Kluwer Academic Publishers, 1999.

Raul H. C. Lopes and Mark Tarver. Inducing theorem provers from proofs. In *ICTAI*, pages 157–164, 1997.

Raul H. C. Lopes. Automatic generation of proof search strategies for second-order logic. In *LNAI vol. 1632, ed. H. Ganzinger, Springer-Verlag Heidelberg*, pages 414–428, 1999.

R. P. Loui. Process and policy: resource-bounded non-demonstrative reasoning. *Computational Intelligence*, 14:1–38, 1998.

Niklas Luhmann. *Rechtssoziologie 1*. Rowohlt Taschenbuch Verlag GmbH, Reinbek bei Hamburg, 1972.

J. Lukasiewicz. *Aristotle's Syllogistic from the Standpoint of Modern Formal Logic*. Clarendon Press, Oxford, 1957.

W. Lukaszewicz. Considerations on default logic. *Computational Intelligence*, 4, 1988.

D. Makinson. General theory of cumulative inference. *Non-Monotonic Reasoning*, 1989.

W. Marek and M. Truszczynski. Computing intersection of autoepistemic expansions. *Logic Programming and Non-Monotonic Reasoning, Proceedings of the first International Workshop*, 1991.

J. McCarthy. Circumscription - a form of non-monotonic reasoning. *Artificial Intelligence*, 13:27–39, 1980.

J. McCarthy. Applications of circumscription to formalizing commonsense knowledge. *Artificial Intelligence*, 28:80–116, 1986.

L. Thorne McCarty. Reflections on taxman: An experiment in artificial intelligence and legal reasoning. *Harvard Law Review*, 90:5, 1977.

Neil McCormick. *Legal Reasoning and Legal Theory*. Oxford University Press, Oxford, 1978.

D. McDermott and J. Doyle. Non-monotonic logic i. *Artificial Intelligence*, 13:41–72, 1980.

M. Minsky. A framework for representing knowledge. *The Psychologi of Computer Vision*, pages 211–277, 1975.

R. C. Moore. Semantical considerations on nonmonotonic logic. *Artificial Intelligence*, 25:75–94, 1985.

T. M. Moussallem. *Fontes do Direito Tributario*. São Paulo: Max Limonad, 2001.

Ilkka Niiniluoto. On the truth of norm propositions. *Rechtstheorie*, 3:171–181, 1981.

K. Nitta, M. Shibasaki, T. Sakata, T. Yamaji, W. Xianchang, H. Ohsaki, S. Tojo, and I. Kokubo. new helic-ii: A software took for legal reasoning. *Proceedings of the 5th International Conference on Artificial Intelligence and Law*, pages 20–29, 1995.

Karl Knut Olivecrona. Realism and idealism: Some reflections on the cardinal point in legal philosophy. *New York University Law Review*, 26:120–131, 1951.

François Ost. Essai de définition et the caracterisation te la validité juridique. *Droit et puvoir. La validité*, 1, 1987.

J. Pearl. System Z: A natural ordering of defaults with tractable applications to nonmonotonic reasoning. In Rohit Parikh, editor, *TARK: Theoretical Aspects of Reasoning about Knowledge*, pages 121–136. Morgan Kaufmann, 1990.

Aleksander Peczenik and Jerzi Wróblewski. Fuzziness and transformation. towards explaining legal reasoning. *Theoria*, 1985.

Aleksander Peczenik. *On Law and Reason*. Kluwer Academic Publishers, Dordrecht/Boston/London, 1989.

Aleksander Peczenik. A coherence theory of juristic knowledge. *A Coherence Theory Of Law*, 1997.

Aleksander Peczenik. Juridiska avvägningar. *Festskrift till Strömholm*, 1997.

Chaim Perelman and Lucie Olbrechts-Tyteca. La nouvelle rhétorique: Traité de l'argumentation. 1958.

Chaïm Perelman and Lucie Olbrechts-Tyteca. *The New Rhetoric. A Treatise on Argumentation*. Notre Dame, Indiana: University of Notre Dame Press, 1969.

Siméon Denis Poisson. *Recherches sur la Probabilité des Jugements en Matière Criminelle et en Matière Civile*. Paris, Bachelier, Imprimeur-Libraire, 1837.

J. L. Pollock. Self-defeating arguments. *Minds and Machines*, 1:367–392, 1991.

J. L. Pollock. A theory of defeasible reasoning. *International Journal of Intelligent Systems*, 6:33–54, 1991.

J. L. Pollock. *Cognitive Carpentry. A Blueprint for How to Build a Person*. Cambridge: MIT Press, 1995.

D. Poole. What the lottery paradox tells us about default reasoning. *Proceedings First International Conference Principles of Knowledge Representation and Reasoning*, pages 333–340, 1989.

Henry Prakken and Giovanni Sartor. A dialectical model of assessing conflicting arguments in legal reasoning. *Artificial Intelligence and Law*, 4:331–368, 1996.

Henry Prakken and Gerard Vreeswijk. Logics for defeasible argumentation. *Handbook of Philosophical Logic*, 2nd ed.:218–319, 2002.

Henry Prakken. *Logical Tools for Modelling Legal Argument. A Study of Defeasible Reasoning in Law*. Dordrecht: Kluwer Academic Publishers, 1997.

Henry Prakken. Dialectical proof theory for defeasible argumentation with defeasible priorities (preliminary report). *Proceedings of the 4th ModelAge Workshop on Formal Models of Agents*, pages 239–253, 2000.

Georg Friedrich Puchta. *Cursus der Institutionen*. in-8vo.Aufl. von Paul Krüger. 2 Bde zus. gebunden, Leipzig: Breitkopf und Härtel, 1875.

Gustav Radbruch. *Gesetzliches Unrecht und übergesetzliches Recht*. in Süddeutsche Juristen-Zeitung, 1, 1946, reprinted in Gesamtausgabe (Collected Works), ed. Arthur Kaufmann (Heidelberg: C.F. Müller), vol. 3: Rechtsphilosophie III, ed. Winfried Hassemer, 1990, 1946.

John Rawls. *A Theory of Justice*. Oxford: University Press, 1971.

Joseph Raz. *Practical Reason and Norms*. Princeton University Press, 1975.

R. Reiter and G Criscuolo. On interacting defaults. *Proceedings of the Seventh International Joint Conference on Artifical Intelligence*, pages 270–276, 1981.

R. Reiter. On closed world databases. *Logic and Data Bases*, pages 55–76, 1978.

R. Reiter. A logic for default reasoning. *Artificial Intelligence*, 13:81–132, 1980.

E.L. Rissland and D.B. Skalak. Arguments and cases: an inevitable intertwining. *Artificial Intelligence and Law*, 1:3–45, 1992.

W. D. Ross. *The Right and the Good*. Clarendon Press, 1930. Oxford.

Alf Ross. *Towards a Realistic Jurisprudence*. Copenhagen, 1946.

A. J. Rover. *Informática no Direito. Inteligência Artificial. Introdução aos Sistemas Especialistas Legais*. Curitiba: Juruá, 2001.

Stuart J. Russell and Peter Norvig. *Artificial Intelligence. A Modern Approach*. New Jersey: Prentice-Hall, Inc., 1995.

Giovanni Sartor. A formal model of legal argumentation. *Ratio Juris*, 7:212–226, 1994.

L.J. Savage. *The Foundations of Statistics*. Wiley, 1954. New York.

Rupert Schreiber. *Logik des Rechts*. Berlin, Göttingen, Heidelberg: Springer Verlag, 1962.

M. Sergot, F. Sadri, R. Kowalski, F. Kriwaczek, P. Hammond, and T. Cory. The british nationality act as a logic program. *Communications of the ACM*, 29:370–386, 1986.

M. J. Sergot. The representation of law in computer programs: a survey and comparison. *Knowledge-Based Systems and Legal Applications*, London Academic Press:3–67, 1990.

G. Shafer. *A Mathematical Theory of Evidence*. Princeton: Princeton University Press, 1976.

G. Shafer. Perspectives on the theory and practice of belief functions. *International Journal of Approximate Reasoning*, 4:323–362, 1990.

Y. Shoham. Nonmonotonic logics: Meaning and utility. *Proceedings of the International Joint Conference on Artificial Intelligence*, Milan:23–28, 1987.

Y. Shoham. Chronological ignorance: Experiments in nonmonotonic temporal reasoning. *Artificial Intelligence*, 36:279–331, 1988.

Jan-R. Sieckmann. The fragmentation of deontic logic. *Paper presented at IVR-03 World Congress on Philosophy of Law and Social Philosophy, Lund*, 2003.

P. Simons. Towards constraint satisfaction through logic programs and the stable model semantics. Research report A47, Helsinki University of Technology, 1997.

Arend Soeteman. *Logic in Law: remarks on logic and rationality in normative reasoning, specially in law*. Dordrecht: Kluwer, 1989.

Wolfgang Spohn. *Grundlagen der Entscheidungstheorie*. Scriptor, 1978. Kronberg/Ts.

Wolfgang Spohn. Ordinal conditional functions. a dynamic theory of epistemic states. *Causation in Decision, Belief Change, and Statistics*, II:105–134, 1988. Kluwer, Dordrecht.

Wolfgang Spohn. A general non-probabilistic theory of inductive reasoning. *Uncertainty in Artificial Intelligence*, 4:149–159, 1990.

Wolfgang Spohn. On certainty. *Lecture on Weltkongress für Soziologie*, 1994.

Wolfgang Spohn. How to understand the foundations of empirical beief in a coherentist way. *Proceedings of the Aristotelian Society, New Series*, 98:23–40, 1998.

W. Steinmüller. Automationsunterstützte informationssysteme in privaten un öffentlichen verwaltungen. *Leviathan*, page 504, 1975.

R. S. Summers. Two types of substantive reasons: The core of a theory of common-law justification. *Cornell Law Review*, 63 n.5:707–735, 1978.

Ilmar Tammelo. *Modern Logic in the Service of Law*. Wien-New York: Springer Verlag, 1978.

Alfred Tarski. A lattice-theoretical fixpoint theorem and its applications. *Pacific Journal of Mathematics*, 5:285–309, 1955.

M. J. Falcon Tella. *Concepto y fundamento de la validez del Derecho*. La Salle, 1998.

Stephen E. Toulmin. The uses of argument. 1958.

Mark Vanquickenborne. Quelques réflexions sur la notion de validité. *Archives de Philosophie du Droit*, 13:185–197, 1968.

Bart Verheij. Reason based logic and legal knowledge representation. *Proceedings of the Fourth National Conference on Law, Computers and Artificial Intelligence*, pages 154–165, 1994.

Bart Verheij. Accrual of arguments in defeasible argumentation. *Proceedings of the Second Workshop, Dutch-German Workshop on Nonmonotonic Reasoning.*, pages 217–224, 1995.

Bart Verheij. *Rules, Reasons, Arguments. Formal studies of argumentation and defeat*. Doctoral Dissertation, Universiteit Maastricht, 1996.

Theodor Viehweg. Topik und jurisprudenz. 1953.

Georg Henrik von Wright. Deontic logic. *Mind*, 60:1–15, 1951.

G. A. W. Vreeswijk. *Studies in Defeasible Argumentation.* Doctoral Dissertation, Department of Computer Science, Free University Amsterdam, 1993.

R. F. Walker, A. Oskamp, J. A. Schrickx, G. J. van Opdorp, and P. H. van den Berg. Prolexs: creating law and order in a heterogeneous domain. *International Journal of Man-Machine Studies*, 35:35–67, 1991.

Max Weber. *Economy and Society.* ed. Guenther Roth and Claus Wittich, Berkeley and Los Angeles: University of California Press, 1st pub. 1922, 1978.

H. P. Williams. Fourier-Motzkin elimination extension to integer programming problems. *Journal of Combinatorial Theory (A)*, 21:118–123, 1976.

Jerzy Wróblewski. The is-ought dichotomy and the naturalistic fallacy. *Review of International Philosophy*, 35:508–517, 1981.

Jerzy Wróblewski. Problems of the naturalistic fallacy. *Synthesis Philosophica*, 5:225–233, 1988.

J. Zeleznikov, G. Vossos, and D. Hunter. The ikbals project: Multi-modal reasoning in legal knowledge based systems. *Artificial Intelligence*, 2:169–204, 1993.

L. Åqvist. Legal wrongfulness as a prerequisite for liability in tort. *Deontische Logik und Semantik*, pages 9–19, 1977.

www.ingramcontent.com/pod-product-compliance
Lightning Source LLC
Chambersburg PA
CBHW061330220326
41599CB00026B/5121